Asleep in th

Asleep in the Deep

Nursing Sister Anna Stamers and the First World War

Dianne Kelly

GOOSE LANE EDITIONS and
THE GREGG CENTRE FOR THE STUDY OF WAR AND SOCIETY

Edited by Brent Wilson and Barry Norris.
Cover and page design by Julie Scriver.
Cover illustration: Adapted from a propaganda poster depicting the German U-boat attack on HMHS *Llandovery Castle*. CWM-19850475-034, George Metcalf Archival Collection, Canadian War Museum.
Frontispiece: Nursing Sister Anna Stamers wearing her working uniform. NANB - Stamers, Anna, Nurses Association of New Brunswick fonds, New Brunswick Museum.
Printed in Canada.
10 9 8 7 6 5 4 3 2 1

Goose Lane Editions acknowledges the generous support of the Government of Canada, the Canada Council for the Arts, and the Government of New Brunswick.

Goose Lane Editions
500 Beaverbrook Court, Suite 330
Fredericton, New Brunswick
CANADA E3B 5X4
gooselane.com

New Brunswick Military History Project
The Brigadier Milton F. Gregg, VC,
Centre for the Study of War and Society
University of New Brunswick
PO Box 4400
Fredericton, New Brunswick
CANADA E3B 5A3
unb.ca/nbmhp

Library and Archives Canada Cataloguing in Publication

Title: Asleep in the deep : nursing sister Anna Stamers and the First World War / Dianne Kelly.
Names: Kelly, Dianne, 1951- author. | Gregg Centre for the Study of War and Society, publisher.
Series: New Brunswick military heritage series ; v. 28.
Description: Series statement: New Brunswick military heritage series ; volume 28 | Includes bibliographical references and index.
Identifiers: Canadiana 20200218387 | ISBN 9781773101767 (softcover)
Subjects: LCSH: Stamers, Anna, 1888-1918. | LCSH: Canada. Canadian Army—Nurses—Biography. | LCSH: Nurses—New Brunswick —Saint John—Biography. | LCSH: World War, 1914-1918—Medical care—Canada. | LCSH: Military nursing—Canada—History—20th century. | LCSH: Llandovery Castle (Hospital ship)—History. | LCSH: Hospital ships—Canada—History—20th century. | LCSH: World War, 1914-1918—Naval operations, Canadian. | LCSH: World War, 1914-1918—Naval operations, German. | LCSH: Saint John (N.B.)—Biography. | LCGFT: Biographies.
Classification: LCC D630.S73 K45 2021 | DDC 940.4/7571092—dc23

MIX
Paper from responsible sources
FSC® C103567
www.fsc.org

Dedicated to the memory of my mother, Donna Parks Christensen,
who was not afforded the opportunity to realize her dream
of becoming a nurse. And to the memory of Anna Irene Stamers,
who was denied the opportunity to return to her home and family.

Contents

Introduction

"Fear now no hope for Nursing Sister Anna Stamers."

This tragic headline appeared in the *Daily Telegraph*, the local newspaper of Saint John, New Brunswick, on July 4, 1918. Anna Stamers, a young Saint John nurse serving in the Great War, was feared lost, along with thirteen of her nursing sister comrades, eighty Canadian Army Medical Corps (CAMC) personnel, and the ship's crew of HMHS *Llandovery Castle*, a Canadian hospital ship. The vessel was returning to England after transporting 644 injured Canadian soldiers to Halifax for convalescence or discharge. On June 20, it left Halifax for Liverpool with 258 persons aboard. According to international law, as a hospital ship, with regulation Red Cross markings and lighting in place, it should not have been a target of war. Yet, on the seventh night of its passage, around 9:30 p.m. (local time), just off the coast of Ireland, a torpedo fired from a German U-boat struck the ship. *Llandovery Castle* sank within ten minutes, and, although some people managed to make it to lifeboats, the U-boat's commanding officer ordered that they be shot. That night, 234 souls died in the cold waters of the North Atlantic.

The losses from *Llandovery Castle* were the highest of any hospital ship the Germans deliberately targeted in the First World War. The sinking was also the most significant naval disaster for Canadians serving in the war. The German officer's order would have far-reaching effects. During the 100 Days Campaign, the last of the war, the deaths of those Canadians would become the rallying cry for Canada's soldiers. Following the war, the actions of the U-boat commander and two other officers became the subject of one of the first war crimes trials, contributing to jurisprudence on the defence of "following a superior's order."

More than 2,800 nurses served in the CAMC during the First World War, of whom more than 2,500 (including Anna Stamers) served overseas. The vast majority of them returned and lived out their lives in Canada, but Anna did not have that privilege. Of the more than 125 New Brunswick nurses who served in the CAMC (see the Appendix), Anna was the only one to die as a result of enemy action. It is important that Canadians, and especially New Brunswickers, know her story.

When Canadian nurses joined up, many had friends, brothers, and other family already serving. They volunteered to provide medical care for sick, wounded, and dying soldiers. They did not expect to die in service. As officers in the military, however, their lives changed in many ways. Before the war was over, for example, they were given the right to vote because of their wartime service. Anna served just over three years in the Great War, from June 3, 1915, until her death on June 27, 1918. She nursed in England and France at large, general hospitals, and ultimately aboard the hospital ship where, at thirty years of age, she lost her life, just four and a half months before the war ended. The details of her service have not been widely recounted, but they are an important part of her story. Her legacy should include not just how she died, but how she served.

Telling her story presents certain challenges for the historian. Anna had two sisters and a widowed mother in New Brunswick, and no doubt they exchanged letters during the three years she served. Unfortunately, only one is part of the public record, a letter Anna wrote in late March 1918, when she was first assigned (taken on strength) to *Llandovery Castle*. Details from this letter were published in the *Daily Telegraph* a week after her death. At that time, families had yet to hear from official sources, and no final list of the victims had been released. In the newspaper's excerpt, Anna listed nine of her fellow nursing sisters and medical officers who were then with her on *Llandovery Castle.* The newspaper printed their names with the caveat, "while this list may have undergone changes on the second and fateful trip, still there is some possibility that it is still fairly correct." The *Daily Telegraph* also published the names of other New Brunswickers who had suffered the same fate as Anna, and those of others who were believed to have survived. Later, families received official notice that their family member was "missing and presumed drowned." Until then, Anna's private letter was used to provide news — any news — to those still desperately seeking word of their loved ones.

Of the more than 2,800 Canadian nurses who served during the Great War, few kept diaries or wrote letters that were published after the war. Taking photographs was against military rules, and letters were subject to censorship within the unit and again before leaving England for Canada. Yet, some found ways around military regulations, and since the centenary of the First World War, more letters and photographs have been published. Among the nurses whose accounts were published after the war, Mabel Clint, Katharine Wilson-Simmie, Elsie Collis, Clare Gass, Sophie Hoerner, Laura Holland, and Mildred Forbes served at the same hospitals as Anna. In some cases, they served before she arrived, but several were with Anna during the same period. Their accounts provide some insight into what daily life was like. If Anna Stamers kept a journal, it would have gone to the depths of the ocean, where she was "asleep in the deep," as one nursing sister later put it. Their voices must speak for hers.

Official records are also available, and many have been digitized. The CAMC maintained official war diaries, and the ledgers and documents of hospitals where Anna served provide a picture of what life was like, and the conditions and challenges that CAMC nurses faced. Using these records, in this book I document Anna's transition from civilian nursing to wartime service, examining the risks, living conditions, and daily routine these nurses encountered. I also connect the fluctuations in demand for patient care to significant battles and the effect that casualties had on the nurses' caseload. Where their diaries and letters offer the nurses' reactions to the strictures of military life, these are included. In many cases, their letters show how faith and friendship sustained them. Anna was from a family with strong religious beliefs, so where these themes are reflected in official documents and/or letters and diaries, I include them.

Anna served for a significant period with No. 1 Canadian General Hospital in Étaples, France, where Colonel Murray MacLaren, a fellow Saint John resident, commanded. Anna no doubt knew Dr. MacLaren, since she had taken her nurses' training at the Saint John School of Nursing, where he had been on staff before the war. The history of No. 1 Canadian General Hospital presents a look inside the daily life of the CAMC and the challenges of providing medical care to the wounded in a series of hospital tents and huts through all kinds of weather. It also documents the significant contribution of nurses from New Brunswick. Anna served with several, both in England and France, and two of her fellow graduates, Nursing Sisters Nellie Floyd and Ethel Moody, were with Anna for most of their service. Unfortunately, their voices, too, are silent.

"The war to end all wars" ended on November 11, 1918, four and a half months after Anna died. Just over twenty years later, another world war followed. Its history has claimed much of our attention, perhaps because many of us have friends and relatives still living who joined up. But in the past one hundred years, technological advances have made service files and official documents available to researchers in ways that First World War participants could never have imagined. Family relationships and citizenship details are accessible through on-line obituaries, immigration records, and census data. Digitization of newspapers from around the world lets us know what they knew and when they knew it. These, together with the official war records, also help to tell the story of Anna's early life and service.

Why should Anna's story be told one hundred years after the event? Perhaps because the enormity of the suffering and sacrifice of those who served in the First World War is staggering. The loss of human capital to a country as young as Canada is incalculable. The grief experienced by Canadians whose children, fathers, brothers, and sisters never came home is now unimaginable. It changed their lives, forever. In the years following the war, Canadians memorialized the sacrifice of those who served.

Nurses were remembered in their schools, churches, local communities, and hospitals, but most of these sites are gone. The Commonwealth War Graves Commission erected a memorial in Point Pleasant Park in Halifax, Nova Scotia, to Canadian men and women who were lost at sea during the First and Second World Wars and who have no known grave. Anna's death is commemorated there. In New Brunswick, the sole remaining memorial to Anna's service is a headstone at Fernhill Cemetery in Saint John.

In this book, I reconstruct Anna's service from official documents and newspaper accounts to tell her story. I also provide historical context and insight into the life and times of young nursing sisters who served during the Great War. Although this is a period now often forgotten, the story illustrates just how much the war changed the role of women, and the opportunities they had as nursing sisters to travel, develop their professional skills, and establish themselves as independent women. I also demonstrate the challenges women like Anna faced integrating into large bureaucratic structures and military nursing, where they had limited control over their lives.

In telling Anna's story, the service and sacrifice of a young New Brunswick nurse, I hope to make the events of a war fought over a hundred years ago more understandable. And, in the retelling, let us remember and appreciate the contribution that Anna and those like her made to Canada's war effort. Lest we forget.

Chapter One

Early Life

Anna Irene Stamers was born in Saint John, New Brunswick, to Benjamin Arthur Stamers and Sarah Lavinia Elliott Stamers. There is no official birth record for Anna, but her military attestation papers give a date of January 15, 1888. In the century that has passed since Anna lived and died, little information remains about her early life. Something of her childhood and education, however, can be gleaned from records of births, deaths, marriages, and obituaries of members of her family held in the Provincial Archives of New Brunswick, as well as census records at Library and Archives Canada and relevant newspaper stories.

From these fragments of the Stamers family legacy, a story emerges of a young woman whose life was marked by tragedy at an early age. Only one of Anna's grandparents—her maternal grandfather—was born in Canada. Her father's parents were residents of the British West Indies and her maternal grandmother was born in the United States. Anna's mother's family came from a more modest background and financial means than her father's side. Anna's maternal grandfather, Elias Elliott, was born in New Brunswick, as was Elias's mother, but his father was born in the United States.

As a young adult, Elias Elliott lived in Westmorland County, where he worked as a blacksmith. While there, he married Anna's maternal

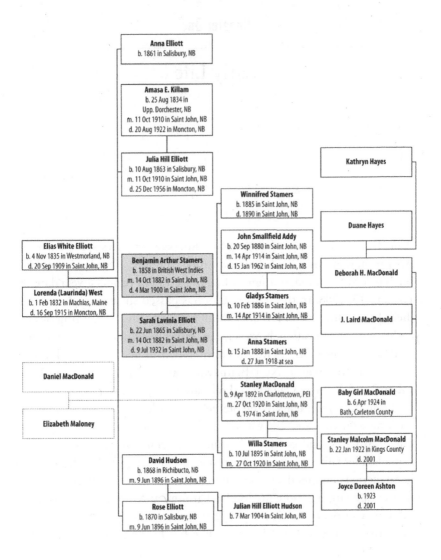

Anna Elliott
b. 1861 in Salisbury, NB

Amasa E. Killam
b. 25 Aug 1834 in
Upp. Dorchester, NB
m. 11 Oct 1910 in Saint John, NB
d. 20 Aug 1922 in Moncton, NB

Julia Hill Elliott
b. 10 Aug 1863 in Salisbury, NB
m. 11 Oct 1910 in Saint John, NB
d. 25 Dec 1956 in Moncton, NB

Kathryn Hayes

Winnifred Stamers
b. 1885 in Saint John, NB
d. 1890 in Saint John, NB

Duane Hayes

John Smallfield Addy
b. 20 Sep 1880 in Saint John, NB
m. 14 Apr 1914 in Saint John, NB
d. 15 Jan 1962 in Saint John, NB

Elias White Elliott
b. 4 Nov 1835 in Westmorland, NB
d. 20 Sep 1909 in Saint John, NB

Benjamin Arthur Stamers
b. 1858 in British West Indies
m. 14 Oct 1882 in Saint John, NB
d. 4 Mar 1900 in Saint John, NB

Deborah H. MacDonald

Lorenda (Laurinda) West
b. 1 Feb 1832 in Machias, Maine
d. 16 Sep 1915 in Moncton, NB

Gladys Stamers
b. 10 Feb 1886 in Saint John, NB
m. 14 Apr 1914 in Saint John, NB

J. Laird MacDonald

Sarah Lavinia Elliott
b. 22 Jun 1865 in Salisbury, NB
m. 14 Oct 1882 in Saint John, NB
d. 9 Jul 1932 in Saint John, NB

Anna Stamers
b. 15 Jan 1888 in Saint John, NB
d. 27 Jun 1918 at sea

Daniel MacDonald

Stanley MacDonald
b. 9 Apr 1892 in Charlottetown, PEI
m. 27 Oct 1920 in Saint John, NB
d. 1974 in Saint John, NB

Baby Girl MacDonald
b. 6 Apr 1924 in
Bath, Carleton County

Elizabeth Maloney

Stanley Malcolm MacDonald
b. 22 Jan 1922 in Kings County
d. 2001

Willa Stamers
b. 10 Jul 1895 in Saint John, NB
m. 27 Oct 1920 in Saint John, NB

David Hudson
b. 1868 in Richibucto, NB
m. 9 Jun 1896 in Saint John, NB

Joyce Doreen Ashton
b. 1923
d. 2001

Rose Elliott
b. 1870 in Salisbury, NB
m. 9 Jun 1896 in Saint John, NB

Julian Hill Elliott Hudson
b. 7 Mar 1904 in Saint John, NB

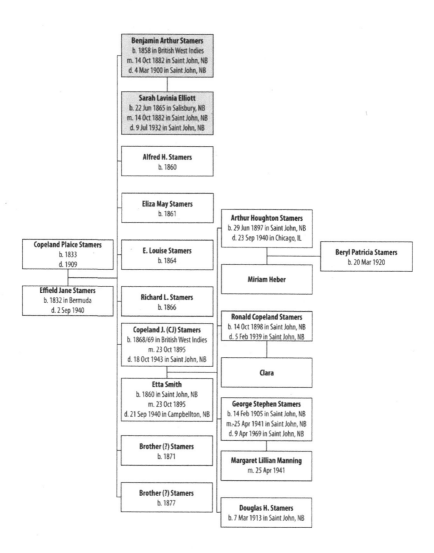

Benjamin Arthur Stamers
b. 1858 in British West Indies
m. 14 Oct 1882 in Saint John, NB
d. 4 Mar 1900 in Saint John, NB

Sarah Lavinia Elliott
b. 22 Jun 1865 in Salisbury, NB
m. 14 Oct 1882 in Saint John, NB
d. 9 Jul 1932 in Saint John, NB

Alfred H. Stamers
b. 1860

Eliza May Stamers
b. 1861

Arthur Houghton Stamers
b. 29 Jun 1897 in Saint John, NB
d. 23 Sep 1940 in Chicago, IL

Copeland Plaice Stamers
b. 1833
d. 1909

E. Louise Stamers
b. 1864

Beryl Patricia Stamers
b. 20 Mar 1920

Miriam Heber

Effield Jane Stamers
b. 1832 in Bermuda
d. 2 Sep 1940

Richard L. Stamers
b. 1866

Ronald Copeland Stamers
b. 14 Oct 1898 in Saint John, NB
d. 5 Feb 1939 in Saint John, NB

Copeland J. (CJ) Stamers
b. 1868/69 in British West Indies
m. 23 Oct 1895
d. 18 Oct 1943 in Saint John, NB

Clara

Etta Smith
b. 1860 in Saint John, NB
m. 23 Oct 1895
d. 21 Sep 1940 in Campbellton, NB

George Stephen Stamers
b. 14 Feb 1905 in Saint John, NB
m. 25 Apr 1941 in Saint John, NB
d. 9 Apr 1969 in Saint John, NB

Brother (?) Stamers
b. 1871

Margaret Lillian Manning
m. 25 Apr 1941

Brother (?) Stamers
b. 1877

Douglas H. Stamers
b. 7 Mar 1913 in Saint John, NB

grandmother, Laurinda West, a woman four years his senior. Laurinda West Elliott was born in Maine, but it is unclear when she became a New Brunswick resident. By the 1871 census, however, Laurinda had had four children with Elias: Anna (ten), Julia (seven), Sarah Lavinia (five), and Rose (one).

By 1881, Elias Elliott had moved his young family to the Kings Head area of Saint John; Anna's mother, Lavinia, was then fifteen. In Saint John, Elias started a new career in the service industry as a hotel keeper, and achieved a level of financial stability for his household. The record of his death in 1909 lists his occupation as hotel manager, although it is unlikely that he was still managing it by then. The Elliott Hotel at 28 Germain Street remained open under that name or as Hotel Elliott until 1921.

Anna's father, Benjamin Stamers, immigrated to Canada from the British West Indies as a young man. Within three years, October 19, 1882, Benjamin married Lavinia Elliott at her mother's family home. They might have met at the local Baptist church, since both families identified as Baptist in census records. Benjamin was then twenty-four and Lavinia just eighteen, but they soon set up their own household.

In 1885, when their first child, Winnifred, was born, Benjamin and Lavinia were living at 117 King Street East. By the next year, when their second daughter, Gladys, was born, they had moved to Union Street. Anna, born in 1888, was the third daughter of four, just as her mother had been in her family. In 1890, just two years after Anna was born, the family's life was marked by tragedy for the first time when the eldest child, Winnifred, died of inflammation of the lungs. By then, the family had moved back to 117 King Street East. Anna's sister Willa, the last of the four daughters, was born on July 1, 1895.

Benjamin Stamers had moved to the port city of Saint John presumably because of his interest in navigation. By the time he married Lavinia, he was the principal of the Saint John Navigation School, a significant accomplishment for a recent immigrant. He had advanced quickly, having received his certificate of competency as "mate" only in 1880. It might be that he had prior navigation training or experience in the British West

Indies and only needed Canadian certification. Nonetheless, by 1881, he had the authority to conduct marine examinations and, although the school was not large, it had students from New Brunswick and Prince Edward Island. He granted certificates to five students in 1881, and took over as proprietor of the school and teacher when its founder died.

Benjamin had been born into a large, influential family in the British West Indies. Anna's paternal grandfather, Copeland Plaice Stamers, was the Assistant Commissioner of Turks Island; her paternal grandmother, Effield Jane Stubbs, was born in Bermuda. They remained in the British West Indies, but others in the Stamers family left for Canada. By the time Anna was three years old, two of her West Indian family members had moved to Saint John: her father's younger brother, Copeland John Stamers, who had emigrated from Turks Island to Saint John in 1888, when he was nineteen, and his sister, E. Louise Stamers. By 1891, the Stamers household consisted of Benjamin, Lavinia; their two daughters, Gladys and Anna; and Benjamin's siblings, Copeland (now twenty-two) and Louise (twenty-six).

Anna's Aunt Louise soon established herself in North America and by 1894 had graduated from nursing at the Boston Homeopathic Hospital. She returned to nurse there following her graduation, and the next year she was appointed head nurse of the institution. The report of her appointment in Saint John's local newspaper described her as the sister of B.A. Stamers. This suggests that, by 1895, Anna's father was well established in Saint John, so much so that his sister's accomplishments and identity were linked to his. Her choice of vocation as a nurse also might have helped to shape the future career choice of her seven-year-old niece, Anna.

By the time she was twelve, Anna had a large extended family living in Saint John. Anna's maternal grandparents resided at 30 Wellington Row, along with her mother's two sisters, Rose (and her husband David), and her Aunt Julia, a spinster. Anna's paternal uncle, Copeland, his wife Etta, and their two toddlers were also living in the city. But her mother's eldest sister, Annie, had married a sea captain and moved away to Parrsboro, Nova Scotia, the year Anna was born, while her Aunt Louise, as we have seen, had moved to Boston several years earlier. It seems, then, that Anna's mother's family were the most influential in her life, since both grandparents and two of her mother's siblings lived nearby.

This was the family's support structure when twelve-year-old Anna and her family suffered another devastating loss. On March 4, 1900, Anna's father, Benjamin, died. According to his obituary in the *Saint John Globe*, he was just forty-two and in the prime of his life. On the day of his death, he had "chatted with his family and dictated several letters," and seemed to be recovering from a leg fracture. His obituary does not say where the family was living at the time, but the 1891 census lists their residence in the Prince Ward of Saint John.

Benjamin, the Stamers family patriarch in Canada, had become an influential figure in Saint John in the twenty years since he had immigrated. At the time of his death, he had a reputation as a thorough navigator and teacher. Besides his roles at the Navigation School, he held a position in the business office of a local Saint John newspaper, the *Messenger and Visitor*. According to his obituary in the *Saint John Globe*, "he took a deep interest in the order of Oddfellows of which he was Past Grand Master. Besides holding the position of Deputy Grand Patriarch in the Grand Encampment he was head of the military branch in Saint John." He was also a member of the Knights of Pythias and the Canadian Home Circle. Actively involved in the local Christian community, Benjamin was a member of the Brussels Street Baptist Church, and "was among the leaders in all departments of its work." In its editorial section on March 7, the *Messenger and Visitor* recorded Benjamin's death with "deep regret and sorrow," noting that he "had given part of his time as assistant in the business department of this paper" and had also "for the past year filled the office of the Maritime Baptist Publishing Company." The editor noted that "Mr. Stamers was a man of unchallenged integrity and truly Christian character, an active and highly valued member of Brussels Street church. To Mrs. Stamers and her family, to whom the blow is a crushing one, we extend Christian sympathy."

It appears, then, that Benjamin was working at three different jobs to care for his family's financial needs, and was well-known in the church and service community. At the time of her husband's death, Sarah Lavinia Stamers, then just thirty-five, was left to raise their three girls on her own. In fact, Benjamin's untimely death created a financial crisis for the young widow. He had died without a will and with very little material wealth to sustain his family. Within weeks of his death, since he died intestate, Lavinia had to apply to the Probate Court to be designated the Administratrix of her husband's estate. Moreover, Benjamin had died with personal property not exceeding $1,500 in value, and "did not die seized or otherwise entitled unto any real estate." He did, however, have a small life insurance policy valued at $1,000 and, as Lavinia attested, a "quantity of household furniture and piano of the value... of about five hundred dollars." Lavinia was obligated, together with her brother-in-law, C. John Stamers, and the insurance agent, to post a bond of $3,333 so that she could be made legal guardian of her three daughters. Before she could access any of the funds, she also had to set aside from the proceeds of the estate an annual sum for the benefit of her three daughters for their maintenance and education until they reached age twenty-one. Finally, after paying $20 in probate fees and posting the bond, Lavinia was made the Administratrix of the estate.

At the time of the 1901 census, the widowed Lavinia, head of her own household, was living in Queen's Ward, Saint John, with her three daughters, Gladys (fifteen), Anna (thirteen), and Willa (six). Fortunately, they now had extended family for support. When Benjamin died, Lavinia's sisters, Julia and Rose, Rose's husband David, and five others were living with the Elliott family, along with a servant, a child, and three other lodgers. This might explain why Lavinia, with three children of her own, did not move in with her parents for financial relief. Rose and David continued to live with Rose's and Lavinia's parents for several years before moving to Glace Bay, Nova Scotia, where David worked as a merchant.

After her father's death, Anna's Uncle Copeland, her father's brother, was the only other significant male role model in her life. When Copeland immigrated to Canada in 1888, the year Anna was born, he initially lived with her parents. Copeland married Etta Smith on October 23, 1895, and was then working for Messrs. Manchester, Robertson & Allison, a large department store established in Saint John in 1866. Together, Copeland and Etta had four children. The census and birth records provide conflicting information on where Copeland and his family lived. The first of the couple's children, Arthur, was born in 1897. At the time, the family was living at 118 Orange Street, Saint John. When Ronald was born in 1898, however, Copeland and his family were living at 171 Waterloo Street, the same address as Anna's family. By the time of the 1901 census, however, Copeland, Etta, and their two children had set up their own household again in another part of Saint John: District 21, Wellington Ward. When a third child, George, was born in 1905, they were back at 171 Waterloo Street. By then, Anna was eighteen and in her last year of high school. It is likely, based on proximity to her aunts and uncle, that in those days she was closest to her mother's sister, Julia, and her father's brother, Copeland, and his family.

Anna's family was not as affluent as those of many of the young women who would become her colleagues in the Canadian Army Medical Corps. As we have seen, her family moved several times within Saint John early in her life, perhaps to receive familial support or to pool their financial resources. At the time of her enlistment in 1915, she gave her home address as 171 Waterloo Street. Understanding the changing dynamics in Anna's family life during her teenage years offers a plausible explanation for why she did not graduate from high school and delayed her entry into nursing school.

Anna was one of four daughters and the only one to pursue a professional career. She completed eleven years of schooling, the norm for that time. However, while Saint John High School has a record of her completing the eleventh grade, she is not listed among the graduates in 1905. It is not clear why. Anna did not enrol in the School of Nursing at the Saint John General Hospital until 1909, almost two years after she first could have done so at age twenty. Four years of her life thus cannot be accounted for with certainty. It might be that, in 1905, Anna was ill or needed to help care for her sister and young cousins. In 1905, her youngest sibling, Willa, was still only ten years old. Her nephew, George, was born in February 1905, the same year she finished school. By then her Aunt

Etta was caring for two other boys, ages eight and seven, in addition to George, and they might have enlisted Anna's help.

What is clear, according to the *Daily Telegraph*, is that, before entering nursing school, Anna spent several years in Nova Scotia living with her Aunt Rose and Uncle David in Glace Bay. Precisely how long is not stated, but the article records that "memories of the brave girl are fondly cherished in this Nova Scotia town." It also says that Anna attended the Glace Bay Baptist Church, where she assisted the pastor, Reverend Dr. Frank Erb, a former Saint John North End boy, as "one of his most dependable assistants." In 1904, Anna's Aunt Rose returned to Saint John to give birth to her son, Anna's cousin, Julian Hill Elliott Hudson, on March 7; perhaps she later went to Glace Bay to help with his care. Anna evidently spent significant time in Glace Bay, and this might account for part of the four-year interval.

Another plausible explanation for the gap is that she was helping to care for her maternal grandparents. By the time she was eligible to enter nursing school in 1908, her maternal grandfather, Elias, quite likely was ill. He died in 1909, at age seventy-four, of senility, and might have required care prior to his death. She also might have had to help her grandmother, Laurinda, who was four years older than her husband, look after him. When Elias died, Anna was twenty-one, a year older than the minimum age for entry into the School of Nursing. She enrolled in the school just two months after his death.

It seems that, by 1909, with her grandfather deceased, her grandmother having moved to Moncton to live with Anna's Aunt Julia, and her young nephew almost of school age, Anna was now at liberty to set her own course.

Saint John School of Nursing residence, ca. 1917. Courtesy of Harold Wright

Chapter Two

The Transition from Civilian
to Military Nursing

Anna began nursing studies at the Saint John School of Nursing in November 1909, and graduated in February 1913. Since Saint John was her hometown, it was the logical place for her to take her training, and because there were no tuition fees, cost was not an obstacle. When she started, the curriculum was a mix of theory and practical instruction, offered over three years. By then, nursing had become an established profession, and some seventy nursing schools were attached to hospitals across the country, including four others in New Brunswick; another three opened in 1917. The profession grew dramatically in the next decade: the 1921 census records that there were 21,162 nurses in Canada that year, up from just 5,476 in the 1911 census.

The Saint John School of Nursing opened on May 1, 1888, as a part of the Saint John General Hospital, which had opened its doors in 1865. The school produced its first nine graduates in 1890, upon completion of their two years of study and practical experience. Although it did not have the status of a university hospital program, it quickly achieved credibility. Several of the first graduates went on to establish training schools in Prince Edward Island; New Glasgow, Nova Scotia; and the Victoria Public Hospital in Fredericton.

Living room of nurses' residence. Courtesy of Harold Wright

Initially, applicants to the nursing school underwent a one-month trial during which they received board and lodging at the hospital. If accepted, they completed a two-year training program. In December 1902, the program was extended to three years and the entry age increased to twenty. To be admitted, applicants had to pass a personality test as proper representatives of their profession, where their behaviour was both prescribed and assessed. The emphasis focused on suitability, character, and willingness to conform to the rules. According to the superintendent, "the true nurse should have health, strength, intelligence, patience, a pure heart and an even temper, cheerfulness, tact, a quick perception and many other qualifications which are necessary to efficiency in her vocation... if she has them not, she has mistaken her calling." Indeed, the school's "Rules for Nurses" set the hours of work, time off, maintenance of their living quarters, and limits on personal visits: "nurses, when off duty, may receive lady and gentlemen friends in the waiting room, at other times, only by permission of the Superintendent of Nurses." This degree of control over their day-to-day lives while in training no doubt eased the transition for these nurses later when they became officers in the Canadian Army Medical Corps. Historian Cynthia Toman argues that once the nursing sisters enlisted, they "moved into an environment that isolated them professionally and socially while inculcating values, beliefs and norms specific to the military."

Student nurses were provided with uniforms and received a nominal sum for clothing and expenses but no compensation during their training. By 1889, after the students had completed a probationary period, they received an allowance of $4.00 per month, increased to $6.00 monthly after the first year and $8.00 monthly thereafter. They did not pay tuition since their instruction was considered as "a full equivalent for their services," and they lived in the hospital or a nurses' residence. As the school expanded, local students were permitted to live at home: student nurse Anna, for example, was living at 171 Waterloo Street at the time of the 1911 census. If they were sent out of the hospital to do private nursing while enrolled as a student, the money received from such services was kept for the benefit of the school.

Shawna Quinn notes that female administrators at hospital-based nursing schools ensured that the quality of on-the-job training and classroom standards was much improved by the 1890s. In 1903, the School of Nursing established a formal curriculum, and Miss Lydia R. Hewitt, the first Superintendent of Nurses, established criteria for written and practical examinations for the student nurses. In 1902, after the nursing program was extended to three years, students were examined on key subjects. Year 1 students studied anatomy and physiology, bed making, taking temperatures, and keeping records. Year 2 covered "material medica," ventilation, hygiene, patient care, making poultices, applying fomentations, bandaging, and cooking and serving foods. In Year 3, their final year, students were examined on general medical and surgical nursing, including anaesthetics, obstetrical and gynaecological nursing, examination of urine and other excreta, hypodermic injections, and names and uses of surgical instruments. Although the focus was on hands-on training, by 1910, when Anna was a student, a room was dedicated specifically as a lecture hall.

Lectures were given at the school on various medical topics. In 1903, Dr. Murray MacLaren, on the staff of the Saint John General Hospital, gave a demonstration and lecture on the use of X-rays; the next year, the topic of his lecture was "The Throat." Over the next several years, lectures were given on "Hygiene and Ventilation," "The Administration of Oxygen," and "Anti-septic Surgery." Two other lectures were devoted to "The Religious Life of the Nurse" and "The Personal Qualifications of a Nurse" — clearly indicating the importance given to the nurses' character.

The first graduation ceremony to recognize the students' accomplishments was held in 1907 and annually thereafter. Anna's mother would have had the pleasure of seeing the first of her four daughters graduate as a young professional. When Anna completed her program in 1913, there were thirteen graduates and the following year, sixteen. Anna's class of thirteen was the largest up to that point and thereafter it never dropped below that level. The Saint John School of Nursing continued to provide opportunities for aspiring nurses until it was integrated into the University of New Brunswick in 1958.

Once she graduated, Anna was a member of a small and elite group of professional Canadian women who could be self-supporting. But these women saw nursing as a calling, not just a profession. Although many of the graduates worked at the Saint John General Hospital, it was also quite common for them to work as private nurses, and this was the choice Anna made following her graduation. Private nursing was not uncommon, but also not well paid. As Maureen Duffus notes, "after three years of training some graduates were still relegated to poorly paid home nursing," where they could be treated almost as servants.

In June 1915, two years after her graduation, Anna signed up to serve with the CAMC. For Anna, improved pay, the status as an officer in the CAMC, and the opportunity to travel overseas were no doubt appealing. As for nursing in a hierarchical system, Anna's only experience was as a student nurse at the Saint John General Hospital while completing her training. This, and the two years she worked as a private nurse, was the extent of her experience when she offered her services to the CAMC.

Many of Anna's colleagues from the Saint John School of Nursing were also keen to serve, and thirty-one graduates of the school did so. Official service files exist for twenty-six of them, many of whom served in the same locations as Anna. In some instances, they overlapped with her in their time of service, but most were not taken on strength until 1916 or later. Consequently, Anna served for a longer period in the war than did most of her colleagues.

At least 125 New Brunswick women served as nursing sisters in the CAMC (see Appendix). By the war's end, more than 2,800 Canadian nurses had served, 2,504 of them overseas in England, France, and the eastern Mediterranean at Gallipoli, Alexandria, and Salonika. The war's impact on the availability of nurses and the growth of the profession was dramatic. According to Desmond Morton, half of all Canadian physicians and surgeons enlisted with the CAMC, and nursing sisters were between one-third and one-half of all trained Canadian nurses. Morton notes that these statistics reflect how badly the nurses were needed: the CAMC's bed capacity grew "from 3,000 beds in June 1915 to over 40,000 in November 1918."

Once Anna and her colleagues were taken on strength, they had little control over any aspect of life. Cynthia Toman notes that the nursing sisters "moved into an environment that isolated them professionally and socially while inculcating values, beliefs and norms specific to the military." There was, however, one significant difference for Canadian nursing sisters when they transitioned from civilian to military practice: they were the only nurses given officer status, and this caused some resentment among the nursing sisters of other medical services. The Canadians took pride in their status as lieutenants. Morton qualifies this, however, saying that "[t]heir rank was Lieutenant Nursing Sister, but this only gave them authority of orderlies and assistants." By making them an integral part of the medical service but not a separate entity, "this ensured that no woman would have authority over a military man beyond the wards." In fact, the women were not referred to as Lieutenant, but rather as Nursing Sister. So, although this was more a pragmatic than progressive decision in this period, it was nonetheless a unique status afforded Canadian nurses. Clearly, the honorific was not one that followed them into civilian life, as it did with many of the men.

Still, having officer status gave the nursing sisters opportunities to socialize with male officers. In several of the larger base hospitals, social activities, including dances, were organized. Major Margaret C. Macdonald, Matron-in-Chief of the CAMC's Nursing Service advocated for the nursing sisters, although this practice caused consternation among her British counterparts, arguing that dancing was a harmless outlet for young women coping with the strains of war. Nonetheless, Macdonald was quite strict concerning their comportment. In a June 2, 1916, letter to the Canadian Director of Medical Services in London, she confirmed that nursing sisters must always wear their working or dress uniforms and not civilian clothing, even when off duty. In this respect, perhaps Matron Macdonald felt that the uniform kept the nursing sisters "in role," which commanded a certain respect.

Their duties were well defined. Toman says nursing work fell into six broad categories of expertise, all of which had to be mastered during the training period: "administrative tasks, responsibilities associated with diagnostic tests, assisting with medical and surgical procedures, performing therapeutic nursing techniques, maintaining and cleaning the wards and equipment, and providing personal bedside care such as bath-

Major Margaret C. Macdonald,
Matron-in-Chief, CAMC.

ing and feeding." These duties were further detailed in the "Instructions for Members of Canadian Army Medical Corps Nursing Service (When Mobilized)." In forty-one statements, nursing sisters were charged with their responsibilities and the behaviours they were expected to demonstrate. They were required to do night duty at least once a month. In addition to nursing their patients in the wards, they were responsible for the "cleanliness, ventilation, lighting, warming, as well as good order of her ward annexes." Nurses were also responsible for record keeping, measuring and controlling the administration of drugs, and controlling supplies, linens, and equipment, including the personal equipment of each patient upon admission. As well, they were expected to train orderlies in nine areas, including cleanliness of the wards, utensils, bandaging, and padding of splints. Nurses were also directed to "show sympathy and kindness" to the friends of those patients on the "dangerous list." Their responsibilities extended beyond the physical care of their patients. They were "earnestly requested to interest themselves in the home circumstances of men being invalided as permanently unfit." They acted as the link between the soldier and the chaplain, and were expected to note the religious affiliation of patients. Finally, nursing sisters were expected to notify the chaplain when one of their charges was seriously ill, and, should the soldier not survive, "reverently" prepare the body for the mortuary.

Record keeping was a major responsibility of the nursing sisters. As Toman notes, they were used to this responsibility in their civilian role, but it was even more critical in wartime: "Records were used to track soldiers through the system, documenting their treatments, medications and progress as well as their deaths." Anna would face this responsibility serving in France, when patients had to be evacuated to England to make room for incoming wounded. Toman points out that record keeping had to be timely because the call might come for patients to be evacuated to England before the next shift. She quotes Nursing Sister Ellanore Parker to describe the role of the sister in charge:

> Often the girls worked far into the next day to dress the wounded and make up the terrible lists of the dead. Books had to be kept and reports made out; each man's name, regiment, religion, relations, wounds, conditions and so on, had to be sent on to the War Office. The charts had to be accurate; the diet list, to draw each man's rations, and the lists for drugs, all came under the jurisdiction of the sister-in-charge. Red Cross supplies, patients' letters, and Ward equipment, all were under her care.

Nevertheless, nursing sisters had to adapt in a time of war. Toman says of the nurses' prior training, "[c]ivilian hospital training programs in Canada had ensured that their graduates were well grounded in the principles of germ theory and scientific management for efficient patient care, principles that formed the basis of standard routines in nursing practice." They faced serious obstacles, however, applying these ideas in wartime conditions. By the time their patients passed through the evacuation chain, they often arrived in muddy clothes with festering wounds. It was not so much that the nature of care given at the front differed; rather, it was, as the official records put it, "the conditions under which caregiving took place on the front" that mattered. And there were other differences. These nurses had to deal with illnesses they had never encountered before, such as gangrene, tetanus, trench fever, and trench foot, which became all too familiar throughout their wartime service.

Another major adjustment for all members of the CAMC, including

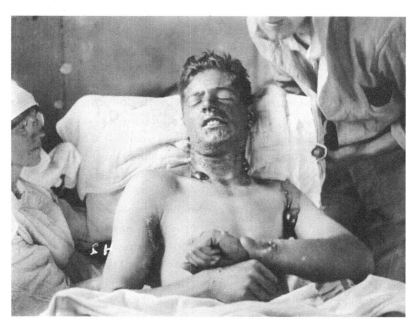

Unidentified soldier with gas burns. Library and Archives Canada / C-080027

the nursing sisters, was understanding the mission of the Corps. Susan Mann describes the role of the nursing sister:

> To repair the wounded, nurse the sick and ease the dying, nurses performed a multitude of tasks. All the ward preparation was theirs, from making and equipping beds to obtaining stores from the central supply, stocking the tiny ward kitchen, and arranging space for the charge nurse to make her reports. The nurses prepared all the dressings, pads of clean cotton gauze, in advance, enough literally for an army. Most of the actual changing of dressings — the replacement of blood-soaked, pus-laden bandages, the washing of the wound with a sterile (and stinging) solution, and its covering up again with a clean dressing fell to the nurses. So too did the feeding of soldiers too weak or

incapacitated to feed themselves. The nurses checked pulses and temperatures, brought down fevers, stopped hemorrhages, and watched for the ever-lurking gangrene.

The role of the nursing sister in the CAMC differed from that in a civilian hospital setting in another way. As Desmond Morton argues, its purpose was neither therapeutic nor humanitarian, but to conserve manpower: the real goal of treatment was to return the soldier to the trenches to fight on once again. This shift in philosophy required an adjustment for physicians and nursing sisters alike.

Early in the war, the nurses confronted terrible injuries, including bullet wounds from machine guns, burns from the German *Flammenwerfer* (flame-thrower), and shrapnel lacerations from exploding shells. In 1915, the Germans introduced chemical weapons in the form of chlorine gas, "about two and a half times denser than air, pale green in colour and with an odour which was described as a 'mix of pineapple and pepper,'" as James Patton relates. The gas reacted with water in the lungs to form hydrochloric acid, which destroyed lung tissue and could lead to death or permanent lung damage and disability. Later that year, the Germans began to use phosgene, a colourless gas that smelled like "musty hay"; because it reacted with proteins in the alveoli of the lungs and disrupted the blood-air barrier, it led to suffocation. The reality was that this war was inflicting completely new types of injuries. Anna nursed patients who suffered from injuries, while learning new methods of medical care and hospital procedures that improved both patient care and outcomes.

Despite their training and experience, nurses faced a completely different environment in the military. Some of the routine was familiar — nursing sisters observed and reported on their patients' conditions and carried out their doctors' orders. Many innovations in hospital admission and discharge procedures, however, had to be established to deal with the huge influx of patients. A new way to cleanse wounds, the Carrel-Dakin method, was introduced and became accepted practice. Blood transfusions also became commonplace by the end of the war, and amputation of limbs was still used to save lives when no other method was viable.

Christine Hallett refers to work in this environment as "containing trauma." The scope of practice ranged from dealing with hemorrhage, sepsis, and the effects of toxic gas to comforting and coping with the dying. As the war progressed, nursing sisters learned how to provide wound care to guard against infection, administer anaesthetics, and to assist in surgeries. As Hallett writes, "[t]he business of military nursing involved daily encounters with dirt, death, pain and despair." These conditions were a major adjustment for the nursing sisters whose work in civilian hospitals had placed great emphasis on cleanliness and hygiene. While orderlies took the responsibility for removing dirty uniforms and washing patients, nurses monitored the patients, cleaned and cared for their wounds, and administered antiseptics. The nurses' main priority was to fight against infection of the soldiers' wounds. As Desmond Morton notes:

> The wounded soldier's worst enemy was infection. Infected wounds produced a bacteria-generated gas with a nauseating stench, monstrous swelling and a dreadful death. French surgeons discovered that gas gangrene could be controlled only by cutting away every fragment of affected flesh and irrigating the wound with a solution of sodium hypochlorite. A typical operation enlarged a tiny infected shell-fragment wound into a hole two or three inches wide, six inches long, piercing deep into a soldier's thigh.

The surgeon could remove the shell fragment and cut away the flesh, but that was insufficient for the wound to heal properly. Because the soldier likely had lain in filth where he was wounded or had fallen while en route with stretcher bearers, wounds quickly became infected. Even when care was needed and the nurse was trained, quality care was not always possible when caseload volumes limited the time nurses had with each patient. For the thousands of victims of poisonous gases, unfortunately nursing care could provide little relief beyond the administration of oxygen. The effects of mustard gas were particularly devastating, stripping the bronchia and burning the skin.

Nursing sisters had to learn to work as a team and carry on in highly dynamic environments. For those, like Anna, whose primary experience was in private nursing, this was a major shift. During her military service, she worked in large general hospitals and in periods of high stress, when the influx of wounded tested the abilities of everyone involved. It was not just the transition to military nursing; it was learning to work in a team environment where following administrative procedures was essential. In the few letters and diaries that exist, some nursing sisters found the formal administrative structures restrictive. It is also clear that they had little appreciation for the complexities of setting up a military hospital in the middle of a war. Even after hospitals were established, they had to learn to cope with expansion and retraction of bed space as the needs arose.

Wartime nursing also had an important psychological dimension both for patients and nurses. When a nurse was present to provide care, Hallett argues, the "comfort" she brought kept the soldier "emotionally and psychologically well, further enhancing physical healing." No doubt this exchange also had similar benefits for the nursing sister when, despite her ministrations, her patient did not recover. She could console herself with the knowledge that, as would later be said of Anna, "she hath done what she could." This attitude was a necessary form of self-preservation for the nurses. Hallett points out that the nurses were required to "contain their emotions" or they would not be able to function.

Military nursing required the nursing sisters to confront death all too often and to help the families deal with the tragic loss of their young loved ones. As Susan Mann expresses it, "[t]he nurses brought lads back from the brink of madness and accompanied them to the edge of death. When the latter took over, the nurses conveyed the soldier's final state and last wishes to his family." Morton identifies the special burden the nurses carried in dealing with death when he states: "Once they completed their surgery or assigned a treatment, doctors could dismiss their patients. Nurses carried on caring for men puffed to double their size with gangrene, stinking beyond a stomach's tolerance, suffering unspeakable

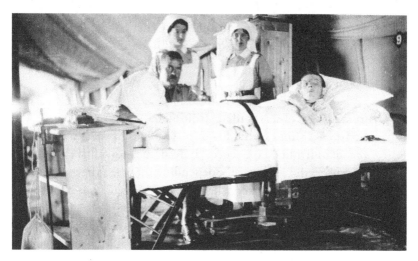

Wounded Canadian soldier in No. 2 Canadian General Hospital with visitor and attending nurses. Edward Kidd / Library and Archives Canada / PA-149305

agony." Sometimes they simply had to find release through expressing their emotions. An Ontario nurse, Katharine Wilson-Simmie, recalled a time when Sister Ross, a colleague of hers from Edmonton, vented her frustration: "Girls, this war is hell, such wrecks of young manhood, just laddies!" As Wilson-Simmie noted, she then "dropped her head on her out-stretched arms and sobbed. We did not try to comfort her, we understood, and her tears relieved the tension."

In the face of these conditions, nursing sisters found ways to cope with the stress of wartime service. Helen Fowlds, a nurse from Hastings, Ontario, described the experience in a letter to her mother in May 1915:

> Well, after that awful week when nobody even smiled, we
> all decided that we had to brighten up and forget it — as
> the war is going to last a long time and worrying won't
> help much....It isn't that we are living in a fool's paradise
> and that we are blinding our eyes to the seriousness of the
> situation but we are here and we've got to stay here and we
> can't help the war by grieving, so we have as good a time as

we can. So, if my letters are rather airy fairy believe me, we all do it — to keep going. You sort of have to forget about the war. It's with us always — like the poor — and requires a poor antidote.

Cynthia Toman observes that, "[u]ltimately, each individual would experience the war from within her own specific context. War was a collective *and* an individual experience." Indeed, the individual experiences of nursing sisters did vary greatly, depending on when they were taken on strength, how long they served, where they served, and, if they were serving close to the line of fire, what was happening at the front when they were there. According to Toman, "war presented an unfamiliar set of circumstances and settings," and she quotes one nurse who said: "Military Nursing follows no law, abides by no rule, is governed by no precedent that is not honored in the breach and disregarded coolly when the occasion, expediency and necessity require." Toman further notes that "a nurse's work was also contingent on the particular hospital unit and ward to which she was posted and on the types of patients treated there." In Anna's case, she would work in several types of hospital setting during her service, and all of them would challenge her in ways she had never experienced in her training or her work as a private nurse.

By the time the war was over, the soldiers fighting in the Canadian Expeditionary Force (CEF) would suffer greatly. Morton records the casualties as 59,544 fatalities, of which 39,488 died in action and 6,767 of disease; a further 13,289 died of wounds or accident. These are sobering statistics. Morton, however, records another significant statistic: 154,362 survived their wounds and illnesses. Their survival was in no small part the result of the work of the CAMC and Canada's nursing sisters — those who made the transition from civilian life to military life, not as a soldier but as a nursing sister. But none of that was apparent when Anna and her colleagues decided to sign up.

Chapter Three

Signing Up to Serve

"When Britain is at war, Canada is at war. There is no distinction." Canada's prime minister, Sir Wilfrid Laurier, made this bold statement to the House of Commons in 1910. Thus, when Britain delivered its ultimatum to Germany, historian Gerald Nicholson writes, Canadians did not question the need to come to Britain's aid. Although most expected that the war would be over by Christmas, it lasted for four long years. Nonetheless, Canada's commitment held. By the time the war ended in November 1918, more than 619,000 Canadians had signed up to serve. At first, on August 7, 1914, Britain's Army Council had asked for one division, consisting of 25,000 men and three field ambulances. Field ambulances typically travelled with the troops, and there was an expectation that nurses would not be placed that close to the front, given their sex and the attitudes in that period. In fact, the initial request specified: "Chaplains and nursing sisters not included."

Within two weeks, the British had revised their requirements. Now, the contingent should include "lines of communication," among which would be medical units that provided care for the wounded behind the battle lines. The British specifically asked for a clearing hospital — later known as a casualty clearing station (CCS) — two stationary hospitals, and two general hospitals. Although initially nurses did not serve in

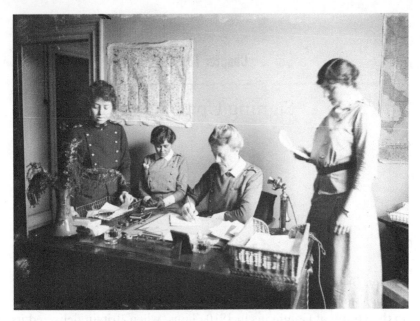

Matron Margaret Macdonald and her staff.
Canada. Dept. of National Defence / Library and Archives Canada

a CCS, they were required to provide care in general and stationary hospitals. The revised request meant that nursing sisters would need to accompany the First Contingent — later renamed the First Division — of the CEF overseas.

Soldiers were already being mobilized in August 1914, and there was little time to recruit the nurses needed to care for the wounded. Canada's Director General Medical Services (DGMS) estimated that as many as 136 nurses would be required to support them. At the outset of the war, however, the CAMC had only thirteen officers and five nursing sisters. Before the war ended, the CAMC had recruited more than 2,800 nursing sisters, 2,504 of whom, including Anna Stamers, served on the Western Front, in Russia, or in the Mediterranean.

Canada's Matron-in-Chief, Margaret Macdonald, the first woman in the British Empire to be granted the relative rank of major, was given the task of screening and selecting who should go from the hundreds of applications she received. She was one of the two full-time nurses of the CAMC at the time. On August 17, she was transferred to Camp Valcartier, Quebec, but it was September 16 before she was advised of the decision to mobilize the nursing service. Before Matron Macdonald could review the applications, the National Association of Graduate Nurses provided a first level of screening. Cynthia Toman says the association "felt professionally pledged to select only nurses who had graduated from a recognized training school when placing their names before the Military Selection Committee headed by CAMC Matron Macdonald." Despite such short notice, Macdonald and her staff proved equal to the task of selecting members. Initially, she identified 119 qualified nursing sisters. From this list, one hundred trained nurses were selected to staff the two general hospitals, fifty nursing sisters for each hospital. When she received the order to mobilize in September, Macdonald had the telegrams ready to notify the candidates.

The candidates had little time to re-spond when informed: "You have been selected as nursing sister for service abroad. You will report Quebec 23rd." Upon receiving this terse directive, the nurses who were selected then under-went a medical examination, and were inoculated, trained for army service, and outfitted in their new CAMC nursing sister uniforms. The Canadian uniforms were quite distinctive, which, according to Shawna Quinn, made the Canadian nursing sisters the envy of the grey-clad

Working uniform worn by
CAMC nursing sisters.
LAC-1970-163, Library and Archives Canada

Imperial and Red Cross nurses. They received both a working and a dress uniform. The working uniform was a light, cornflower-blue cotton dress and tunic with twin rows of brass military buttons down the front, over which the nurses wore a fitted white apron. The apron was held in place by a Sam Browne leather belt.

The dress uniform was navy-blue serge, with a high round collar and cuffs edged with scarlet. Depending on the weather, nurses wore either a navy-blue, long military coat, high black boots, and black stockings, or a navy cape lined in scarlet. Katharine Wilson-Simmie, who sailed for England in May 1915, described her pride in wearing her uniform: the epaulettes on the shoulders were "fitted with two First Lieutenant's stars, indicating our rank in the Army Medical Corps."

Kenneth Cameron notes that each nursing sister was allocated a grant of $100 for her uniforms, a significant sum in the period. Both uniforms drew comment, especially the colour of the Canadians' working uniform, which led to Canada's nursing sisters being called Bluebirds. The dress uniform was somewhat militaristic, and Wilson-Simmie recounted an instance where, when they arrived in London, an elderly woman asked, "Excuse me please, but are you policewomen?" The fact that the nursing sisters held the rank of lieutenant, with such a distinctive uniform, led to some consternation on the part of one English medical officer, who asked Wilson-Simmie, "So, are you two stars up? Why do you wear the Sam Brown belt?" Wilson-Simmie grew impatient after several of these comments, and replied: "This is the Canadian Army Medical Corps uniform. I am proud of it and trying very hard to be worthy of it."

Of the one hundred nurses who were notified of the acceptance, ninety-six were able to report as ready to board the SS *Franconia*, together with the matrons, Margaret Macdonald and her colleague, Ethel Blanche Ridley, and the men of the 90th Winnipeg Rifles. The remaining four nurses made their way to England separately and joined the group there. On October 3, the *Franconia* was one of a convoy of thirty-two ships carrying the First Contingent that left Canadian waters. Although their original destination was Southampton, they arrived in Portsmouth on October 14.

Four nurses from New Brunswick were on the *Franconia*: Theodora McKiel, Dr. Margaret Parks, Catherine Hare, and Mabelle Jamieson. Those who were the first selected were considerably older and presumably had more experience than other nurses in the province. By the end of the war, more than 150 nursing sisters with a New Brunswick connection had served in the CAMC (see the Appendix). Of these, twenty-four were graduates of the Saint John School of Nursing, the school that Anna attended.

The nurses were keen to do their part. They had the same fear as the men who signed up: the war might be over before they got their opportunity to serve. The day following the declaration of war, the Director-General of the CAMC, Colonel Guy Carlton Jones, addressed the Ottawa Graduate Nurses Association. He tried to temper their enthusiasm, cautioning the women about the differences between civilian and military nursing. "Many nurses who will do for civil work are physically and mentally unfit for active service work." According to Colonel Jones, three qualities were required for the arduous work of army nursing: "Coolness, courage, and skill to serve where many wounded and dying are constantly being brought into the field hospital." As Quinn notes, the other requirements were more quantifiable: candidates had to be between twenty-one and thirty-eight years of age, graduates of recognized nursing schools (Canadian training schools were preferred), and members in good standing. For most nursing schools, the entry age was twenty-one, which meant that graduate nurses volunteering to serve with the CAMC were at least twenty-four when they applied. Later, the requirement was added that nursing sisters must have trained at a recognized Canadian hospital that had, as Morton says, "not less than 100 beds." Presumably, war experience taught recruiters that nurses who had worked under a formal administrative structure in a larger facility were better able to adapt when patient intake and turnover were high.

Canadian nurses were not easily dissuaded by Colonel Jones's words, and hundreds of applications poured in. Some women elected to make their own way to England to join the Queen Alexandra's Imperial Military Nursing Service (QAIMNS), or the Red Cross, or to serve with the French, fearing they would not be accepted into the CAMC before the war ended. Like many of the men who signed up, nurses were motivated to serve for many reasons, including a sense of adventure. Others saw it as their duty to support the Mother Country, since many had immigrated to Canada from Britain. It was also an opportunity to develop themselves professionally. The fact that they would have officer status might have been another factor. For others, the prospect of financial security was appealing in a period of high unemployment. According to Morton, in 1914 even many family doctors were struggling financially, since many of their patients lacked the resources to pay for their services. Presumably, the inability of patients to pay was also a problem for private duty nurses such as Anna.

Nurses who had already chosen a "helping" profession were also likely influenced by wartime propaganda that appealed for their assistance. They might have imagined themselves in "heroic and sacrificial roles," although in time the strain of nursing and the nature of the injuries they encountered led to disillusionment for many nurses, just as it did for the soldiers. Many of them also had brothers, cousins, and other relatives who had signed up. Serving sometimes became a family endeavour, and enlisting enabled these women to share in that experience and to visit their siblings while the war was on.

The need for medical personnel quickly increased. By July 1915, 419 nursing sisters were supporting the CAMC in France alone, the number rising to as high as 828 in 1918. Before the war ended, Canada supplied three casualty clearing stations, four stationary hospitals, fourteen general hospitals, seven special hospitals, eight convalescent hospitals, two hospital ships, and various other services of the medical corps. To support these facilities, the CAMC leadership determined that an establishment of 1,528 medical officers, 1,901 nursing sisters, and 15,624 other ranks would be needed to serve the wounded, exclusive of reinforcements.

Some of those who served overseas later required a less stressful posting in England or back in Canada, but Matron Macdonald never had a shortage of applicants, even as the war progressed. She later stated: "the voluntary supply of trained nurses from Canada was at all times in excess of the need" — in 1915, she had 2,000 applicants for 75 positions. Rather, Matron Macdonald's challenge was to manage the resources and decide on placement, matching the abilities of the nurses to fluctuations in demand.

At the outset, Matron Macdonald had more applications than were needed to staff the two general hospitals being sent in 1914. The list they prepared in October, entitled "Canadian Expeditionary Force, Nursing Sisters," included the names of 119 applicants. Only 100 were taken on strength that fall to serve with the First Contingent. Since so many had applied, Macdonald prepared a second list of applicants. The names of the 19 applicants included on the October 1914 list who did not sail in October were carried over to the 1915 Reinforcing Drafts Nominal Roll. This list named 130 who would be given the opportunity to become a nursing sister with the CAMC that year. It is not clear when the nurses were informed that their names were on the Reinforcements list, but on January 22, 1915, they began to be taken on strength and given their opportunity to serve. Further intakes followed: on February 24, forty nursing sisters were taken on strength in London; on June 3, a further fifty were enrolled in Montreal. Anna was part of the Montreal group.

In 1915, many nursing sisters who joined up were part of fully staffed medical teams from university-based hospitals. The names of the eminently qualified nursing sisters from these hospitals do not appear on the 1914 initial list or on the Nursing Sisters, Reinforcing Drafts Nominal Roll, 1915. Presumably, these nurses were not screened by Matron Macdonald, as this was a separate agreement entered into with the Minister of Militia and Defense, Sir Sam Hughes.

Many of the young women who signed up with the CAMC were from privileged, affluent households, with connections that helped them be among the first to be taken on strength in 1914 and 1915. Others, however, came from a range of family backgrounds: middle class, as well as urban and rural working classes. Whether privilege and social connections mattered for selection, many of the nurses who served nonetheless did have that advantage. Katharine Wilson-Simmie had a cousin who worked for Sir Sam Hughes, and was taken on strength in May 1915, although her name is not on the Reinforcements list. As Wilson-Simmie related, she received a telegram from her cousin stating, "Contingent of Nurses being Compiled Stop Do you wish to go?" "Did I wish to go! Nothing on earth could have stopped me once I was on my way to the telegraph office with my reply." It appears that her willingness to serve and her contact in the office of the minister of defence were all she needed, as she was told shortly thereafter, "Hold yourself in readiness for further orders."

No doubt there were others whose contacts allowed them to jump the queue. Mildred Forbes, who crossed paths with Anna, came from a well-connected family in Quebec, including the Tuppers and Gaults. Her brother from her father's first marriage became a doctor and founder of the Montreal Memorial Children's Hospital. Her Quebec colleague and friend, Laura Holland, had a brother who was secretary of the Board of Trade. Like Anna's, however, both Mildred Forbes's and Laura Holland's names were on the 1915 Reinforcements list.

Anna's family was not as affluent as those of many of her colleagues, and she probably did not have many special connections. Her father had been dead for fifteen years before she joined the CAMC. However, Dr. Murray MacLaren, one of the physicians who had lectured at the Saint John School of Nursing, had been appointed Commanding Officer of No. 1 Canadian General Hospital (CGH), one of two general hospitals established in 1914. Anna ultimately would serve fifteen months at No. 1 CGH in Étaples, France, initially while Dr. MacLaren was still CO. It is not known if this connection worked to her advantage.

The Militia and Defence Files provide the details about Anna's selection. She began the application process for acceptance into the CAMC on February 4, 1915, when she signed her application for a position. When anyone received word of their acceptance in the CAMC, newspapers immediately reported it. On February 5, the Moncton *Daily Times* records that five New Brunswick nurses "have won the competitive distinction of going to the front... Miss Graham, Campbellton, Miss Woods, Welsford, Miss McKeen, Rothesay, Miss Babbitt, Georgetown [*sic*,

(opposite): Attestation paper of Anna Stamers. Library and Archives Canada / LAC-B9225-S032

ATTESTATION PAPER

No.

Folio.

CANADIAN OVER-SEAS EXPEDITIONARY FORCE

QUESTIONS TO BE PUT BEFORE ATTESTATION.

(ANSWERS)

1. What is your name? *Anna Irene Stamers*
2. In what Town, Township, or Parish, and in what Country were you born? *St John St John N.B. Canada*
3. What is the name of your next-of-kin? *Mrs J. B. Stamers*
4. What is the address of your next-of-kin? *171 Waterloo St John N.B. Canada*
5. What is the date of your birth? *Jan. 15th 1882*
6. What is your trade or calling? *Graduate Nurse*
7. Are you married? *No*
8. Are you willing to be vaccinated or re-vaccinated? *yes*
9. Do you now belong to the Active Militia? *No* *yes*
10. Have you ever served in any Military Force? *No*
    If so, state particulars of former Service.
11. Do you understand the nature and terms of your engagement? *yes*
12. Are you willing to be attested to serve in the CANADIAN OVER-SEAS EXPEDITIONARY FORCE? *yes*

Anna J. Stamers (Signature of Man.)

M. H. Forbes (Signature of Witness.)

DECLARATION TO BE MADE BY MAN ON ATTESTATION.

I, *Anna Irene Stamers*, do solemnly declare that the above answers made by me to the above questions are true, and that I am willing to fulfil the engagements by me now made, and I hereby engage and agree to serve in the Canadian Over-Seas Expeditionary Force, and to be attached to any arm of the service therein, for the term of one year, or during the war now existing between Great Britain and Germany should that war last longer than one year, and for six months after the termination of that war provided His Majesty should so long require my services, or until legally discharged.

Anna Irene Stamers (Signature of Recruit.)

Date *June 2* 1916   *M. H. Forbes* (Signature of Witness.)

OATH TO BE TAKEN BY MAN ON ATTESTATION.

I, *Anna Irene Stamers*, do make Oath, that I will be faithful and bear true Allegiance to His Majesty King George the Fifth, His Heirs and Successors, and that I will as in duty bound honestly and faithfully defend His Majesty, His Heirs and Successors, in Person, Crown and Dignity, against all enemies, and will observe and obey all orders of His Majesty, His Heirs and Successors, and of all the Generals and Officers set over me. So help me God.

Anna Irene Stamers (Signature of Recruit.)

Date *June 2* 1916   *M. H. Forbes*. (Signature of Witness.)

CERTIFICATE OF MAGISTRATE.

The Recruit above-named was cautioned by me that if he made any false answer to any of the above questions he would be liable to be punished as provided in the Army Act.

The above questions were then read to the Recruit in my presence.

I have taken care that he understands each question, and that his answer to each question has been duly entered as replied to, and the said Recruit has made and signed the declaration and taken the oath before me, at *Montreal* this *2nd* day of *June* 1916.

(Signature of Justice.)

I certify that the above is a true copy of the Attestation of the above-named Recruit.

Major (Approving Officer.)
N.26

M. F. W.
640 M. B-1.
H. Q. 1772-39-595.

Gagetown], and Miss Dickie, River Charles." Yet, none of these names was on the Reinforcements list for 1915. If Anna read this account, the absence of her name must have been disheartening, as she was so eager to go. In the interim, documents were forwarded confirming that Anna was approved by the military, that she was a graduate of a recognized school of nursing, and that she had completed her medical. On April 24, she received a telegram addressed to 11 Orange Street, Saint John, asking, "If selected, will you accept appointment. Wire Reply." Anna replied the next day, confirming, "I will accept appointment with expeditionary forces." Then, on May 13, almost three and a half months later, she received a telegram confirming that she had finally been accepted in the CAMC. Two of her friends and colleagues from the Saint John School of Nursing, Ethel Moody and Nellie Floyd, were also accepted. They would travel together.

Acceptance into the CAMC was a coveted accomplishment, and the news was quickly reported. On May 1, the *Daily Gleaner* reported: "Saint John and Fredericton volunteers ordered to hold themselves ready," and listed Anna, Ethel, and Nellie, as well as a "Miss Winslow" of Fredericton. When Anna received the official confirmation on May 13, it stated, "You have been accepted to proceed for duty with overseas contingents.... You will report immediately to ADMS [assistant director medical services], 4th Division, Militia HQ Montreal." She was advised to travel light: "If you have an AMC uniform, take it. Your luggage is limited to one steamer trunk, one handbag or hold all." As if to underscore her change in status to a military nurse, the telegram concluded with the statement: "Transport requisition will be forwarded to you. No civilian clothing required." Anna replied by telegram the same day, stating, "Will report Montreal as directed."

Again, the news of their final acceptance spread quickly. On Saturday, May 15, the Saint John *Standard* reported that the three local women had been accepted and "will leave for Montreal on Monday night." On May 18, the Moncton *Daily Times* reported that Anna, Ethel, and Nellie had, the previous day, left on the Ocean Limited train for Montreal, where "they will sail for overseas duty." The paper confirmed that many friends and members of the Red Cross Society were at the depot to wish them goodbye and shower them with gifts. Anna was identified as the niece of Mrs. E.A. Killam, Highfield Street. On May 29, the *Daily Gleaner* gave a long list of nursing sisters as "those who have gone or are going from the Maritime Provinces." It included Anna, Nellie, and Ethel from New Brunswick, as well as Irene Barton and Margaret Fearon under the heading "others going." The same article listed the names of women recruited to go with university-based hospitals that had sent complete medical teams in 1915. Ruth Loggie from Burnt Church, New Brunswick, and Clare Gass of Shubenacadie, Nova Scotia, were listed as assigned to "the General," No. 1 CGH.

Several other New Brunswick nurses on the Reinforcements list were taken on strength in May 1915 and got to France before Anna. Florence Mary Armstrong and Joyce Wishart from Saint John were assigned to No. 1 Canadian Stationary Hospital (CSH) on March 11. On May 11, however, they were transferred back to London and did not return to France. Nella Wilson of Saint John was taken on strength at Le Touquet on May 13. On May 1, Alice Powers of Saint John was taken on strength, and Nellie Donohue and Nella MacDonald from the Saint John School of Nursing joined No. 1 CGH on May 12.

On May 29, 1915, a *Daily Gleaner* headline reported: "Patriotic women flock to front as nurses," and cited Montreal as "the centre from which patriotic women have left for the front as nurses, and from which many more will go. From all over the Dominion, women who wish to engage in this work, are flocking to Montreal, where every facility is offered them in the carrying out of their ambition." The story continued: "Fifty nurses are now mobilizing at local militia headquarters from all over Canada.... Following are the names of the nurses from the Maritime Provinces who have left and those who are going." The article then listed those nurses going from "No. 3 General Hospital" and "From the General," including Clare Gass and Ruth Loggie. The article also listed "Red Cross Nurses," Dr. Armstrong's group, and finally "Others going also," including Anna, Ethel, and Nellie, together with Irene Barton and (Irene) Margaret Fearon. On May 29, the *Moncton Transcript* published a letter from Nellie, Ethel, and Anna, written on May 15 from the Queens Hotel in Montreal and addressed to the Moncton Loyalist Protestant Band:

> We the three St. John nurses for overseas duty wish to thank you for playing for us on arrival at your station. We appreciated it very much. Your music surely cheered us on our way and we hope very much to hear you play again, and hope it may be when we come home again.

On June 4, Anna sailed from Montreal on the RMS *Metagama* as part of a group of fifty nurses whose names were on the 1915 Reinforcing Drafts Nominal Roll. Before they departed, however, a series of prerequisites had to be met. In addition to having inoculations, a medical examination, and fittings for their uniforms, the nurses attended a series of lectures on military nursing. Their service files show that some of the nursing sisters had their inoculations in Canada, while others completed them during the voyage. The process took about a month. Nova Scotian Clare Gass—who served at two of the same hospitals as Anna and kept a

RMS *Metagama*. CC_PH_03014, Chung Collection, University of British Columbia Library

Nursing Sisters Anna Stamers, Nellie Floyd, and Ethel Moody.
NANB - Military 15, Nursing Association of New Brunswick fonds, New Brunswick Museum

diary of her experiences in adapting to military nursing—received notification that she was to serve with No. 3 CGH (McGill) on March 4. Her diary entries show that, after reporting for duty, the nurses had a series of lectures on military nursing and received the typhoid vaccine in three doses over a period of seventeen to eighteen days. During this interval, she and her colleagues ordered their uniforms, provided by William St. Pierre Limited, 41 Union Street in Montreal, and returned for fittings about three weeks later. Just the day before sailing for England on June 4, they made their attestation, and Anna, Ethel, and Nellie had a studio portrait taken of them in their working uniforms.

Other administrative details were also completed. Now that Anna was officially a nursing sister in the CAMC, she was on the payroll. Nursing sisters were paid $2.00 per day plus field, messing, and travel allowance. On a monthly basis, nursing sisters were paid $60.00, plus $18.60 for field

Nurses who sailed for England on the RMS *Metagama*, June 4, 1915,
under the supervision of Acting Matron Mildred Forbes.
Top row (left to right): Nursing Sisters Benire, Campbell, Barton, Beatty, Mitchell,
Code, Whelan, Best, Templeman, Watson, McLaughlin, Brady, Murton,
Telford, Walter, Sampson, McKenzie, Taylor, Glasgow, Ruddick,
Howard, McDermott, Refoy, Groves.
Bottom row (left to right): Reynor, DeLacy, Fearon, Lamplough, Holland, Mowat,
Cameron, McDonald, Aitkin, McLean, Forbes, Maguire, Cookson, Floyd,
Stamers (circled), Moody, Hamilton, Bell, Whitteck, Morrice, Seely, Jukes, Lamiter.
Courtesy of New Brunswick Museum

duty and $30.00 for "messing"—their food allowance. Anna, like most of
the nursing sisters, sent a significant portion of her earnings home.

Anna's contingent of nursing sisters was under the supervision of
Mildred Forbes, who served as acting matron of the group until they
reached England and could be assigned. When Anna was finally taken
on strength at Montreal on June 3, Forbes had signed her attestation
papers as well as those of others in the group. Laura Holland, Mildred's
friend and confidante, was also part of the group. Both Mildred and Laura
frequently wrote letters to friends and family during their service, which
were later published as *War-Torn Exchanges*. These letters provide details
on the sailing date, the ship, the crossing, and when and how they were
received on arrival in England.

Before leaving Montreal, the entire group of nursing sisters posed
for a photograph on the grounds of McGill University. The photo of the
women in dress uniform was published in a newspaper and later given

to the New Brunswick Museum. There is no information concerning who the donor was, when the photo was donated, or the name of the newspaper that published it. However, the names of the nursing sisters are listed under the photo and match those of the fifty from the Nominal Roll, with a few exceptions. Arabella Gregory, Elizabeth Ryan, and Ella Willett are not in the photograph, although one of them might be the person who took the photo.

For Anna and her friends, crossing the Atlantic would be their first introduction to the risks of military nursing. The nurses typically travelled with troopships, just as the first group had done in 1914, but the conditions in 1915 were now more perilous. On February 16, the Germans declared a naval blockade around Great Britain, threatening with U-boats all who crossed the Atlantic.

Katharine Wilson-Simmie left Ottawa for Halifax by train, and sailed aboard the RMS *Hesperian* on May 1, 1915. As she later reported, while travelling their windows were blacked out and rules were strictly enforced against smoking or lighting matches on deck. In fact, while they were under sail, the nurses and soldiers were required to wear their life-belts day and night. They were later told that the *Lusitania*, a British passenger ship, had been torpedoed and sunk by a German submarine. Two Canadians were among those lost: James Dunsmuir, son of former British Columbia premier James Dunsmuir, and Nurse Eleanor Charles, a 1913 graduate of Vancouver General Hospital. They had been aboard the *Lusitania* en route for military service in Britain. The loss of so many lives in the sinking of the great liner was a seminal event in 1915, and moved the United States closer to joining the war. The attack also caused the captain of the *Hesperian* to alter his route to ensure safe passage, and affected the sailing of every ship crossing with troops and nursing sisters thereafter.

Another Canadian nursing sister, Sophie Hoerner, who served with No. 3 CGH (McGill), travelled across the Atlantic just before Anna and also wrote home about her voyage. When she sailed on the RMS *Metagama* from Montreal on May 7, there were 104 nurses from three hospitals (McGill, Laval, and Kingston) on board. In a letter written that day, Sophie confided her fears: "We heard about the *Lusitania*. Got a wireless and it was posted up. Made us all think a good deal." Later in the trip, on May 12, Sophie wrote, "Everyone is glad it is rough for they say the submarines can't get us. We have two British cruisers ahead of us."

Anna and her friends nonetheless crossed without incident, and nine days later, on Sunday evening, June 13, the *Metagama* reached Plymouth. Initially they were not allowed into the port. Laura Holland wrote that they were taken ashore by tender the next day. She described their experience on arrival in a critical tone: there was no one at the harbour to meet them, and "there were fifty of us waiting on the platform." As matron in charge, Mildred Forbes made inquiries, and they were directed to take the train to London. After walking half a mile to the station, they had lunch on the train, travelling in the first-class section. On arrival, again there was no one to meet them, but finally they were accommodated at two hotels, the Kingsley and the Thackery. Presumably, someone arranged for their personal effects to be delivered, as they had each been allowed a steamer trunk and handbag.

Over the next month, Forbes worked with Matron Macdonald to place the nursing sisters. Again, Laura Holland expressed her exasperation at the delays, this time at not being able to immediately get to work: "It seems funny when one hears of the amount of work to be done in France that they have so much difficulty finding places for us—but evidently nothing is done in a hurry; on the other hand, we might be sent off on six hours' notice." Holland and Forbes made the best of their free time while waiting for Forbes's responsibilities as acting matron to be completed. When not working, the two shopped, visited Buckingham Palace, St. James's Park, and Piccadilly. Two other nursing sisters from Saint John who had arrived earlier also enjoyed seeing the sights of London. Shawna Quinn records that Joyce Wishart and a colleague used their time to tour Buckingham Palace, the Tower of London, and the Guildhall, and attend a symphony at the Royal Albert Hall. Katharine Wilson-Simmie's memoir notes that the nurses were billeted at the Kingsley Hotel in Bloomsbury Square: "For most of us, it was a first visit to old London." Likely, it was also the first trip to London for Anna and her friends. After arriving on

June 13, Anna, Ethel, and Nellie had more than two weeks before they received their assignments. No doubt they, too, explored London and its surroundings.

Anna knew that her family would be concerned about her safety crossing the Atlantic, so, when they arrived in England, she cabled her aunt to confirm their safe arrival. On June 15, the Moncton *Daily Times* headline told everyone else: "Cable to Mrs. A. E. Killam from her niece, Miss Stamers, says they landed at noon on Monday." The article reported that they had arrived at Plymouth, but incorrectly identified their ship as the *Megantic*. However, and more important, the *Daily Times* reported, "Friends in Moncton and elsewhere will be glad to hear that the trip across was made safely." On July 6, the paper reported that nurses in London had "called last week at the office of the New Brunswick government," and listed them as "Anna J. Stamers, Ethel K. Moody, Margaret L. Fearon, Nellie C. Floyd and Lena M. Barton."

When Mildred Forbes's administrative duties were complete, she and Laura Holland were assigned to the Duchess of Connaught Hospital on the Cliveden estate near Taplow, and never served again with Anna. Their letters help to confirm how Anna travelled to England and that she likely had some recreation time on arrival. Official documents tell more of Anna's early story overseas. The Militia and Defence Files contain the official confirmation of when and where Anna was assigned on arrival in England, and a document on her service confirms that she was at Moore Barracks at the Shorncliffe Military Camp, near Folkestone, Kent, from July 2, 1915, to February 19, 1916.

Anna was one of 636 nursing sisters who began their service in 1915. Matron Macdonald and Matron McCarthy, Matron-in-Chief of British troops in France and Flanders, decided who served where, based on who was available to meet the need for care. Synchronizing the recruitment and deployment of medical staff with the construction or conversion of existing buildings into hospitals was challenging. So was caring for the wounded.

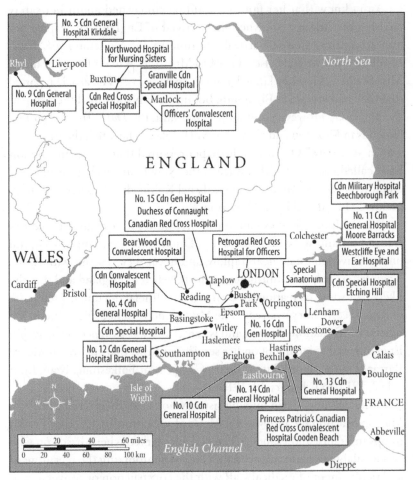

Army hospital locations, southern England and Wales. Mike Bechthold

Chapter Four

Nursing in the Canadian Army Medical Corps: Moore Barracks

Anna Stamers began her service in the Canadian Army Medical Corps on June 3, 1915, and continued until her death on June 27, 1918. Before her life ended, she worked at two general hospitals in England, a large general hospital in France, and a hospital ship. Each of the hospitals had its own culture and differed in its emphasis on social activities to keep up morale. Although Anna left no personal account or letters describing her work, war diaries, records of service, newspaper reports, and letters and diaries of other nursing sisters give form and shape to the story of Anna's experience as a wartime nursing sister.

On July 2, 1915, Anna began her first assignment at Moore Barracks, near Folkestone, Kent, where she served for about eight months before moving on to France. By then, the CAMC had become fully committed to the war effort both in Britain and in France, Belgium, and the Mediterranean. The CAMC personnel who left Canada later in 1914 to support 1st Canadian Division initially included staff for one casualty clearing station, two stationary hospitals, and two general hospitals, all to be established in France. This was thought to be an adequate establishment to support the Canadian sick and wounded. But, since Canadian soldiers were not ready to move to the front until February 1915, only No. 2 Canadian Stationary Hospital (CSH) went to France, on November 6, 1914, becoming the first Canadian military unit to cross the Channel. In France, it opened in a hotel in Le Touquet, near Étaples, with three hundred beds; the first patients were British soldiers suffering from trench foot.

In the meantime, the troops and remaining CAMC staff of 1st Division moved from Salisbury Plain to better facilities at the Shorncliffe Military Camp, near Folkestone, Kent. Shorncliffe became the staging centre for Canadians travelling to and from the Western Front for the rest of the war. When 1st Canadian Division went to France in February 1915, No. 1 CSH and No. 1 Canadian Casualty Clearing Station (CCCS) went with them. No. 1 CSH set up at Wimereux, on the French coast about twenty-five miles north of Étaples. When the Canadians engaged in their first battle at Neuve Chapelle in March, No. 1 CCCS and No. 1 CSH were available to provide care for the wounded.

The first real test for the Canadians came at the Second Battle of Ypres in Belgium, in late April. Nothing could have prepared the Canadians for the carnage they encountered. During the battle, 5,500 Canadians were killed, wounded, or went missing. Field ambulances cared for 10,403 casualties from Canadian and other forces. Of these, 79 officers and 1,983 other ranks were Canadians, representing 20 percent of the casualties. Much of the care was provided by the staff of No. 1 CCCS, Nos. 1 and 2 CSH, and No. 2 Canadian General Hospital (CGH), which had been established in March at Le Tréport, farther down the French coast from Étaples. Andrew Macphail, in his official history of the Canadian forces in the war, says the experience of Second Ypres proved that the medical service was organized and competent—in fact, it "came into actual being at Ypres as a living and powerful force." In May, No. 1 CGH, under the leadership of Saint John's Dr. Murray MacLaren, crossed and established themselves at Étaples. By the end of that month, the CAMC had two Canadian general hospitals, two stationary hospitals, and two casualty clearing stations supporting troops on the Western Front.

By early 1915, it was already evident that more medical support would be required in England for convalescing soldiers. Moore Barracks Military Hospital was one of the hospitals established to meet this need. Located close to the English Channel, Moore Barracks began operations in May 1915, a month before Anna and the nursing sisters of the Canadian reinforcing drafts arrived. From May 4, 1915, until September 13, 1917, it operated as a British hospital, staffed by Canadians, under the command of Colonel Wallace A. Scott, whose war diary notes that the Barracks also included the Auxiliary Hospital, Queen's Canadian Military, Beechboro Park and, in 1916, was given responsibility for the Isolation Hospital and Smallpox Hospital at Folkestone. Later in 1917, Moore Barracks was designated as No. 11 Canadian General Hospital.

Macphail writes: "The original intention was that the British service should care for the serious cases at Tidsworth or in Salisbury but the influx of wounded from Ypres filled up those centres and the Canadians were obligated to provide for their own. The Imperial Authorities decided to allot Moore Barracks to the Canadian Authorities for hospital purposes." According to the Record of Service for Moore Barracks, once this decision was made, the British took responsibility for making the necessary alterations and structural changes, and to supply all barrack equipment. The Canadian authorities agreed to provide the technical equipment and the necessary personnel. This shared arrangement became a source of frustration and preoccupation throughout 1915 for Colonel Scott. Moore Barracks had been set up primarily to accommodate sick and injured soldiers from Canadian camps in Britain, and secondarily to receive sick and injured from France. Patients were also received from many other sources: the first were ninety-eight soldiers transferred from No. 1 CGH when it moved to France in early May.

By the time Anna arrived at Moore Barracks in July 1915, the hospital had become part of a well-developed medical hierarchy. Three Canadian general hospitals were already set up along the coast in France at Étaples, Le Tréport, and Boulogne, about forty miles behind the front lines in Flanders and northern France. No. 1 CGH was situated at Étaples because of its good drainage, accessibility by road and rail, and its strategic location near the port of Boulogne. These locations allowed quick access to the coast for patient evacuation to England, and enabled those who had recovered to be reintegrated into the front lines.

Unloading a stretcher from an ambulance.
CWM 19920044-811, George Metcalf Archival Collection, Canadian War Museum

When Canadian soldiers were wounded or became sick, they were assessed for care or "triaged" — a complex, efficient military procedure, first developed by the French, that both dictated how incapacitated soldiers would be moved from the front lines and where the resources to treat them were located. The Canadian War Museum explains that triage was "a selection process to determine which patients would be operated on immediately, which could wait a few hours, and which were untreatable and, therefore, would be left to die. It was a harsh but necessary system."

Gerald Nicholson describes the triage process used to evacuate soldiers from the front lines. The first line of support were the trained medical officers of the CAMC's Field Ambulances. They were the closest to the line of fire, about two miles away, and the first point where, when night fell, the walking wounded or those carried out by stretcher bearers could be assessed. Behind them was the CCCS, which could take as many as two hundred patients, but initially had no beds and no nursing sisters. Both the Field Ambulance and the CCCS were intended to be mobile

Canadian nursing sisters at Moore Barracks, Shorncliffe, England, ca. 1918.

enough to move with the troops. Behind the CCCS was the stationary hospital, equipped with two hundred and fifty beds and sixteen nursing sisters. The name stationary hospital was a misnomer in that it was also expected to move as needs changed. Farthest from the front was the base hospital or general hospital, staffed by a matron and seventy-two nursing sisters, with a capacity to handle five hundred or more wounded, and later expanded up to two thousand beds. When a battle resulted in a high number of casualties, injured soldiers sometimes bypassed points in the evacuation chain because of the volume of cases.

The original intention was to keep the nursing sisters out of harm's way by keeping them farther from the front. When Mildred Forbes worked at a casualty clearing station, she explained the process to her friend in a letter: "The CCS are quite far up the line — it is the nearest that women get to the front without any danger of course to any of us… I mean we are safe there yet as close to things as women are allowed." By 1917, this practice was abandoned when air raids on stationary and general hospitals made the distinction moot and the volume of cases and nature of care demanded it.

Moore Barracks was not a purpose-built hospital. According to the Record of Service, it consisted of "forty-seven buildings, five of which were two storey... [M]any alterations to these buildings were necessary and many temporary buildings and huts were erected, also some canvas." The hospital and adjoining staff lines sat on the cliffs overlooking the Channel, making it a vulnerable location, situated as it was in proximity to the CAMC Training Depot and close to Folkestone port. The echoes of artillery fire carried easily across the water. Diane Beaupré describes the reaction of a twenty-three-year-old Winnipeg soldier on his first day after arriving at Shorncliffe: "We could hardly believe our ears. I don't know about the other fellows, but it was a queer feeling through me to know that only 50 or 60 miles away, our boys were fighting and dying. Before this, the war seemed very unreal, but the sound of the guns made me realize that it was a grim reality and I wondered how I would face it when the time came."

Working there in 1915, Anna also had the unnerving experience of air raid warnings. Being in England did not mean that the nursing sisters and medical staff were out of harm's way. Maureen Duffus writes about a British Columbia nurse, Elsie Collis, who had been at Shorncliffe for only about two weeks when she experienced the terror of an air raid. Her diary entry on October 12 records: "an air raid six miles away, three men in our hospital, fourteen killed." According to Duffus, Canadian soldiers were killed in air raids at Shorncliffe on three occasions. The hospital's Record of Service confirms that they had "numerous warnings of air raids and many times enemy aircraft passed over the hospital and dropped bombs." One fell inside the hospital lines and wounded a person. The hospital also cared for many casualties from air raids. In 1915, it received thirty-six wounded, twenty-two of whom died, and in 1917, ninety-eight wounded, of whom twenty-seven died. Colonel Scott's war diary entry for November 5, 1915, states:

Lights are now put out throughout the entire Hospital at 7:00 p.m. This is on account of the fact that we are in such a prominent position and any light showing can be seen for a considerable distance out at sea. Although blinds have been placed throughout the entire Hospital it is found that from time to time lights do show even though the blinds are drawn and to avoid any difficulty on this score the order to hâve the lights extinguished at 7:00 p.m. has been given.

Clearly, during the summer and fall of 1915, although she was not yet at the front, Anna and her colleagues lived with the ongoing threat of injury or death. Nevertheless, Duffus describes Elsie Collis's service at Shorncliffe as "a gentle and uneventful introduction to wartime nursing," since it was close to London's attractions: sightseeing, theatres, galleries, and shopping. Whether or not Anna had the opportunity to take advantage of their proximity to London is not clear.

For much of the time that Anna was at Moore Barracks, the hospital was under construction, as efforts were made to unite the forty-seven separate buildings into a functioning hospital. This affected every aspect of their working lives and their living conditions. Most of Colonel Scott's war diary entries focus on the administrative challenges of converting barracks into wards, dining halls, recreation halls, and an operating room. Moore Barracks operated without an X-ray machine for the entire time Anna worked there. The lack of such a unit preoccupied Scott, who was frustrated that patients had to be taken to Shorncliffe Military Hospital for the procedure. Working in a series of separate buildings was also difficult, and in February 1916, the roads between the buildings were in very poor condition. As Scott noted on February 3, "[a]lmost as soon as the rain comes the main roads through the Hospital become a pool of mud."

Anna and her colleagues did not live at Moore Barracks when they first arrived. In fact, it was likely as much as six weeks before they lived on-site. On August 18, Scott's diary noted: "The nursing sisters who have been billeted in Folkestone up to the present time, moved into their new quarters at Moore Barracks today. There [*sic*] present quarters are satisfactory and placed more conveniently for work. Alterations are still being made in these quarters but should be completed shortly." Either he was optimistic, or there might not have been room for everyone to move on-site. On August 31, he listed the outstanding work on the hospital and wrote: "Progress in the Nurses' quarters is slow, lines are being placed throughout the hospital and this work is very slow indeed." Then, within two and a half months, the nursing sisters were likely returned to billets, but Scott's diary entry on November 14 is not clear on this: "Ward 29 was closed to Nursing Sisters as it was found that the accommodation was required for the patients." From the war diary, it appears, that, although Scott preferred the convenience of having the nursing sisters living and working on-site, by November 1915 the pressures of accommodating the sick and injured had taken priority. His diary entries for the period that Anna remained there do not record the nursing sisters returning to live at Moore Barracks.

Working conditions at Moore Barracks were difficult for many reasons. The continuous construction meant moving patients within wards and elsewhere throughout the camp. Colonel Scott's diary entries beginning in August 1915 reflect the challenges of converting a military barracks to a functioning hospital while caring for 540 patients. On August 5, the Drill Shed was converted into a Dining Hall and Recreation Room, and on August 6, he noted that an annex was being constructed to connect the Kitchen to the Dining Hall. On August 7, he recorded that "the alterations being made to Wards 1 to 6 are almost complete and should soon be occupied." On August 8, he noted: "the post-operative ward will soon be ready for occupation." Patients initially accommodated in Wards 7 and 8 were moved to Wards 5 and 6, while Wards 7 and 8 were "turned over to the Engineers for alteration and renovation." By mid-August, the Post-Operative Ward was opened, and by August 27, his diary entry confirms that "the Operating Room floor is almost complete...numbers of the new wards opened." On August 31, he noted that "the new wards opened are excellent, the only difficulty being the narrow doors to the passages which makes it difficult to carry a stretcher." Diary entries in October confirm that, by mid-month, work was still under way by the engineers to reconstruct the wards, and on October 14, Ward 31 was opened as a Post-Operative Ward. Wards were still being constructed into November. During all this construction, the demand for patient care continued unabated. On October 27, Scott noted: "Opened a new ward with 37 beds." On November 1: "Ward 12 was handed over to us today by the Engineers is equipped for 37 beds. It was no sooner opened than a number of patients arrived and were admitted straight away into this additional ward." By this point, 603 patients were in care. Despite this, Scott's diary entry on November 4 noted: "I inspected the repair work being done by the Engineers and found progress to be satisfactory, although slow. The Wards that they are altering for occupation are urgently required and we are still having a number of patients who have to be sent to the Military Hospital for disposal." Construction simply could not keep up with the demand for beds.

On December 8, Scott noted that, "owing to the considerable number of patients still arriving from the various lines, it is necessary to evacuate patients to either Convalescent Homes or elsewhere at the rate of 60 patients per day." While work continued to establish an X-ray room, Scott recorded on November 18: "Arrangements have now been made with the Shorncliffe Military Hospital whereby we can commence taking X-ray pictures when necessary. We have to supply our own Assistant Radiographer but a great difficulty now has been overcome." His preoccupation with access to X-rays suggests that the soldiers requiring care had not simply fallen ill, but rather were seriously injured, although his diary entries provide no insight into the nature of the cases. Anna and her colleagues, in short, had to cope with changing living conditions, working in a noisy and changing workspace, and with very limited tools available to assess a patient's needs.

Moore Barracks had limited recreational activities for soldiers who were convalescing and for medical staff who were caring for them. On August 29, Scott confirmed that a "Service of Song" was given in the Recreation Room by a number of local people and "was greatly appreciated by the men." Their enjoyment, however, was short-lived. Inclement weather and the lack of adequate heating made the Recreation Room and Dining Hall so unpleasant that the facilities were not used — it was just too cold on the coast of Kent. On November 1, Scott noted: "Two stoves which have been placed in the Dining Hall and one stove placed in the Recreation Room have been found insufficient and an Ident has been sent for three additional stoves in Dining Hall and either a fireplace in the Recreation Room or an additional stove. At present neither the Dining Hall or [sic] the Recreation Room can be comfortably heated."

The local population helped. On November 7, Scott recorded: "Arrangements are now made whereby cars, privately owned by people desirous of showing their appreciation of the services rendered by patients, call every afternoon for the purpose of taking a number of men for drives through the District. These drives are greatly appreciated." On November 24, he wrote that arrangements were made for a fully equipped Recreation Room with money taken from the Company funds. "This Recreation Room should prove of great value in making men who are employed here more comfortable when out of actual duty hours. The hours off duty, however are few." Just two days later, Scott's entry confirmed that "[c]oncerts are from time to time held in the Recreation Room but the cold is too severe to allow of these being the success they should be. As previously stated there is only one stove in this room. The Recreation Room is not so comfortable as it might be, were there some fund from which to draw in order to make this room more attractive it would be good." His entry on December 1 reflects the lack of progress, despite his best efforts: "Although considerable amount of correspondence has been exchanged on the subject of sufficient heating for the Dining Hall and Recreation Room, nothing so far has been done."

Inadequate heating was not limited to the Dining Hall and Recreation Room. On December 14, Scott noted that "[c]oal oil stoves have been secured for the use of bronchitis patients. This has been found absolutely essential." Despite their best efforts, life at Moore Barracks for the nursing sisters and their patients did not include much recreational activity in 1915.

On February 17, 1916, the issue of appropriate heating in the Dining Hall and Recreation Room made its way to the floor of the British House of Commons. Hansard records an exchange between Member of Parliament Francis Bennett-Goldney and the Under-Secretary of State for War, Harold Tennant, on that date. In his remarks, Bennett-Goldney called on the under-secretary to address the lack of heat in the Dining Hall and Recreation Room where the Canadian soldiers were suffering from both neglect and indifference. He stated that:

> large numbers of suffering convalescent men, many of them striving to recover from pneumonia, rheumatic fever, and lung trouble, have been compelled to sit in this shelter, sometimes in an atmosphere barely distinguishable from the raw mists without; seeing that this state of things is likely to continue unless some notice is taken in London of the representations which have been put forward again and again since the beginning of December by the medical authorities concerned through the usual channels, will he say what action he proposes to take?

According to Bennett-Goldney, the Imperial engineer officer at Shorncliffe "has been absolutely forbidden not merely not to have the stoves fixed himself, but not to permit the Canadian engineers to fix them." Tennant's response makes clear that action was finally taken at Moore Barracks. As Hansard for February 17, 1916, records,

> No dining room existed at Moore Barracks, so the Drill Hall was allotted for this purpose, with the approval of the local military medical officers, both Canadian and British. Two stoves were first installed, and as these were found inadequate, three more have since been added by the War Department, making five in all. The building (designed as a drill hall) necessarily lacks some of the comfort of an ordinary dining room. No reports have been received at

the Headquarters, Eastern Command, from the general at Shorncliffe or the medical officers concerned that the heating now provided was inadequate. I am asking for a special report on the accommodation of which complaint is made.

From this intervention, it appears that, by mid-February, the matter of heating "now provided" in these rooms had been resolved, although Scott's diary does not confirm this.

Scott gives little detail about changes in staffing and inconsistently records the names of individual nursing sisters when there were changes in staffing. Instead, he focused his attention on changes in officers, or when dignitaries visited. On August 4, General Sir Sam Hughes, the Minister of Militia and Defense, and the Honourable Andrew Bonar Law and Sir Max Aitken—both New Brunswickers who were members of the British Parliament—visited, and Scott recorded that they "expressed satisfaction with the general condition of things here," noting that Bonar Law addressed the troops in the Drill Hall that evening. In mid-November, he recorded an inspection by a Major Caun, who "examined everything and stated that he considered the progress of the hospital marvelous and that when the natural difficulty of converting barracks into a hospital were taken into consideration, Moore Barracks Hospital compared favorably with any hospital he had examined." While this perspective might have been correct, it did not lessen the adjustment for the nurses as they transitioned from civilian to military nursing in a time of war.

Scott made a few references to religious services. On December 5, he recorded that church services were being held "on each Sunday" for the patients in the Patients Recreation Room: "Mass being held at 6:30 a.m. and Holy Communion held at the small Chapel at the same time. Divine Service commences at 10:30 and Holy Communion at 11:30 a.m. Confessional being held between five and seven p.m. in the small chapel." Despite the cold of the Recreation Room, the soldiers and nursing sisters must have considered spiritual support a priority.

Working in such an environment was challenging. By fall, tension had escalated between the nursing staff and the medical officers over their respective roles. On October 28, Matron Macdonald visited and met with Colonel Scott. His diary entry suggests that they conversed about this thorny issue, and no doubt Macdonald met with the nursing staff. He recorded: "Definite instructions were given prohibiting the nursing sisters from in any way encroaching on the work of the Medical Officers." Whether this was a widespread problem or not, Scott chose to address it with Macdonald and note it for the record. Perhaps some needed a reminder of the rules. Susan Mann notes that the nursing sisters had to abide by a set of instructions "for members of Canadian Army Medical Corps Nursing Service when mobilized," which listed forty-one statements concerning the responsibilities and conduct expected of nursing sisters. The last two were: "She will be careful to exercise due courtesy and dignity in all her relations with officers, N.C.O.s, men and patients," and "She will bear in mind that unquestioning obedience and loyalty to her superior officers are an obligation." This was yet another adjustment the nursing sisters would have to make as they transitioned to military nursing.

Like all Canadian nurses, Anna's previous experience had been in a civilian hospital with a relatively stable patient caseload. There the work environment was clean, safe, and fully equipped to provide the necessary level of care. Working as a military nurse in the CAMC required a major adjustment. Nursing sisters had little or no control over their living conditions or work environment. Sophie Hoerner chafed at these restrictions when she first arrived in England. Writing to her mother in May 1915, Sophie vented her frustration: "We are now like machines. Are not allowed to think for ourselves.... There is a certain amount of excitement in not knowing what you are going to do next. It is so queer and strange for me. I have always run my own affairs and known what it is I wanted to do. Now, I am being run and don't know anything."

The fact that Anna spent her early days billeted in Folkestone and only part of the time living in converted barracks might have been fortuitous. No doubt the living conditions in the billets were more comfortable than the wards would have been in the early winter of 1916. Nonetheless, the working conditions in the wards and other buildings became even more uncomfortable as the season progressed. Scott's war diary entries feature few references to social events that involved the nursing staff and medical staff together. In any case, his legitimate concerns about the risk of air raids left little opportunity for socializing in the evenings. Moreover, it appears that, at Moore Barracks, Scott encouraged a clear distinction in roles and ranks.

Little is known about Anna's first Christmas at Moore Barracks. Colonel Scott noted on November 30 that an application had been made to the ADMS to arrange for Christmas for the patients. The local people and the Red Cross Society offered their support for celebrations: "Some 200 are entertained by local tradesman but as there will be some 800 men in hospital, other arrangements will have to be made for 600 men." A concert was held on December 24, and the next day each patient received a Christmas stocking and had Christmas dinner in the Dining Hall and wards, each "suitably decorated." Scott's war diary does not record whether the nursing sisters had any role in organizing the festivities or participating in them. Since they had been billeted in the community for at least part of the year, they might well have been invited to homes in the community. Likely, this will have been the first Christmas Anna spent away from her family, just as for the soldiers in her care.

When Anna and her colleagues arrived at Moore Barracks in July 1915, they had little idea about the range of adaptations they would have to make. Of the group that travelled together from Canada, Wilhelmina (Mina) Mowatt, a nursing sister from Manitoba, served with Anna at Moore Barracks until they were transferred to France. When Anna and Mina arrived, the whole of Shorncliffe Military Camp was a hive of activity, and its Canadian staff was derived from a number of recruiting initiatives. In 1915, universities with nursing programs organized their own hospital units, starting with McGill. Others followed: Victoria, Toronto, Queen's, Western, Manitoba, Dalhousie, Laval, and St. Francis Xavier sent entire medical units, including nursing sisters. These "general hospital units" were assigned briefly to Shorncliffe Military Camp while en route to France and the Mediterranean. No. 3 CGH stayed from mid-May to mid-June before moving on to France; No. 5 CGH Victoria stayed from September 5 to November 16 before moving on to Salonika in Greece.

Depending on when they arrived, the nurses' caseload demands varied. Elsie Collis was one of forty-five nursing sisters from the Royal Jubilee Hospital in Victoria, British Columbia, assigned to No. 5 CGH, who served briefly at Moore Barracks in the fall of 1915 while Anna was there. Her diary shows her impatience with the organizational challenges and the fluctuations in workload at Moore Barracks in this period, while she waited to sail to the Mediterranean. From early October until she left in December, the number of incoming patients ebbed and flowed. "Sunday, October 3, 1915 Had a convoy (wounded troops) come from France," the second in two days. Then, on October 7, Elsie "Left Moore Barracks for Central Military, down the hill. Our unit taking it over, an awful muddle. No one knows anything about the place." There must have been another convoy, because the next day she wrote, "very busy, two boys with fractured backs. Some very sad cases. Poor things you long to do something for them." The pace of patient intake must have picked up by the fall during Anna's time there. According to the Record of Service, before the end of 1915 Moore Barracks admitted 9,127 patients in the eight months after it opened. At first, it was staffed and equipped for 520 beds, but by 1916 its capacity had nearly doubled to 950 beds.

Moore Barracks was not alone in its frequent case turnover. The number of patients in hospital on any one day at any of the hospitals fluctuated with the rhythm of the war, as the nursing sisters soon discovered. As Desmond Morton writes, "a year's cruel experience indicated that a modern war produced masses of casualties, but in floods or trickles." As the war progressed, more and more hospitals were set up. Even once established, hospitals had to expand and contract to handle the fluctuations in demand for care. One of Canada's three essential contributions to the war effort, according to Morton, along with "the training and dispatch of reinforcements to replace casualties, [and] the organized training and dispatch of additional units and formations," was to rehabilitate the sick and wounded for further service. This was the reality of military nursing.

Like Elsie and Sophie, Anna had to adjust to this functional outlook, the constant shifting demands for patient care, and the limited freedom of military life.

The war diary for Moore Barracks does not provide details about the nature and types of injuries of patients. While Anna served there, the hospital received patients from France, both British and Canadian. In the period June to December 1915, which was most of the time Anna served at Moore Barracks, No. 1 CGH sent 7,051 patients from Étaples to England. Moore Barracks would have received many of them, and Kenneth Cameron's history chronicles the flow. According to Cameron, even in 1915, No. 1 CGH functioned as "an enlarged better equipped, more stable and supposedly safe Casualty Clearing Station. The pressure from the front was so great at times that patients were only held until they gained sufficient strength to enable them to be sent to England or had recovered and were transferred to a convalescent depot or to duty." Almost half of the patients at No. 1 CGH in that period were admitted with wounds (5,079) and the remainder (5,525) as a result of disease. Once transferred to Moore Barracks, patients still required significant care before they could be considered convalescent.

Anna and her colleagues at Moore Barracks treated soldiers who required more long-term care or who required further surgeries. They had to ensure that any hint of infection did not result in setbacks. As Christine Hallett notes, watching for infection was an essential task for nursing sisters, as "wounds easily became infected and in a pre-antibiotic era, infection was highly dangerous and often fatal." Nursing sisters quickly became competent in recognizing that a wound had become unhealthy when its colour became greenish yellow or when its discharge became dark brown or red, and even by its "offensive, even putrid smell." Nurses such as Anna had never before encountered these kinds of wounds. In many cases, the patients had had limbs severed or removed to preserve their life. As Morton points out, however, "despite the terrible injuries caused by modern war and the septic soils of France and Flanders, 93 percent of those who reached treatment survived their wounds."

Cameron says "the destruction caused to the human body by shrapnel and other weapons" in June 1915 was so bad that, in four days, nearly 400 were admitted, mostly without passing through a casualty clearing station. "They had first aid and anti-tetanus serum [provided by the Field Ambulance] but the filth had not been removed from their persons nor the foreign bodies from their tissues," and many had suffered "ghastly suppurating wounds." During this period, of the 1,074 treated at No. 1 CGH, more than half were evacuated to England. "During the first two weeks of July, the great number of casualties from the trenches of Hooge [near Ypres in Belgium] called for large numbers of admissions and discharges." The fighting about Hooge continued until mid-July, when there was a lull. Cameron notes that the types of wounds were severe, and twenty-six men died. Injuries included wounds to the head, and "on active days, eight skulls were opened to remove missiles." In July 1915, 1,065 were admitted and 850 evacuated to England. In August, the types of wounds were especially severe from burns when the Germans introduced the use of the *Flammenwerfer* (flame-thrower). Of the 1,261 admitted, 486 were transferred to England.

The month of September at No. 1 CGH Étaples proved to be very quiet up until the twenty-fourth, when "orders were received not only to clear as many as possible, but to increase bed capacity by 500 so as to make the total capacity of the hospital 1,500 beds." Cases were increasing and more patients were presenting with injuries. Cameron notes that, although the injuries required surgery, these wounds were caused by bullets, and the penetration resulted in clean wounds. In September, of the 1,675 admissions, 1,019 were wounded; October's statistics were similar. The majority of these were evacuated to England: in September 1,270 and in October 1,272. The diary for Moore Barracks reflects a steady increase in the number of patients during this same period. Based on Cameron's description, it is likely that those who had surgery were sent to England to recover. Anna would have cared for men at Moore Barracks who had suffered some horrific wounds, even if they had their initial surgeries done in France.

According to Christine Hallett, the type of care the nurses provided had positive effects on the well-being and survival of patients. She notes that the care included "the dressing of wounds, the positioning of a patient to prevent pressure sores, the maintaining of cleanliness and hygiene, the provision of nutritious food and adequate fluids and the offering of reassurance...these were part of the art of nursing." Nurses were expected to focus on their patients as "whole beings," rather than on their specific diseases. Hallett argues that, in so doing, the practice of nursing enabled the wounded to become as well as possible during the treatment regimen.

Throughout 1915, the transfer of cases from France to England continued, resulting in high caseloads for Moore Barracks. The cold and damp of the fall in France made November the month of trench foot and trench fever. The majority of these cases—1,307 of the 1,993 patients admitted to No. 1 CGH—were evacuated quickly to England. Clearly, long periods in the trenches were taking their toll on the soldiers, and the need for care shifted dramatically. This pattern continued through December, when, of the 1,913 admissions, 1,247 were admitted due to disease and 1,341 evacuated to England.

In February 1916, at the end of Anna's service at Moore Barracks, Matron C. Russell completed a performance appraisal of her work. The document, held in her Militia and Defence file, was a standard form with space for remarks. The appraisal provided for assessment of Anna's performance in two main areas: Nursing Capabilities and Administrative. Nurses were rated on their tact, zeal, judgement, personal conduct, and general fitness. Matron Russell rated Anna's performance as "good" in all these areas. She did not provide any other remarks on Anna's overall performance. Apparently, Russell considered Anna's performance satisfactory, and Anna was considered sufficiently capable and competent for transfer to nursing soldiers at the front. By then, Anna had gained valuable experience in treating soldiers suffering from war-related illnesses and injuries. In her next assignment, she would care for patients who were much closer to the front lines and who would need her care more immediately after their wounding.

Chapter Five

Service in France at
No. 1 Canadian General Hospital

Across the Channel, meanwhile, at the Canadian general hospitals near Étaples, 1915 had been a difficult year. Clare Gass, from Shubenacadie, Nova Scotia, was temporarily assigned to No. 1 CGH at Étaples, and her diary provides insight into life at a major hospital in France during these early days before Anna Stamers arrived.

Clare — who shared a room with Ruth Loggie of Loggieville, New Brunswick, during her service in France — and her colleagues arrived at Boulogne en route to Étaples on May 18. She described her first impressions: "The road is one constant stream of ambulance waves with the wounded. In fact, it seems to be for all practical purposes an English town, there are so many soldiers about its streets." No. 1 CGH did not open for patients until May 31 and, as Clare related, "[n]othing is ready yet for work but the actual tents." The Étaples Administrative District (EAD) consisted of four camps for hospital units, three with huts and one with tents. When presented with their accommodations, Clare's initial impression was that "our tents are very comfortable. Ruth and I are together in one of the larger ones." The hospitals were constructed on the coast, which made movement of the wounded to hospital barges convenient, but offered no natural protection against the unpredictable weather. Within a few days, her view of life in a tent changed: "May 23. Did not sleep very

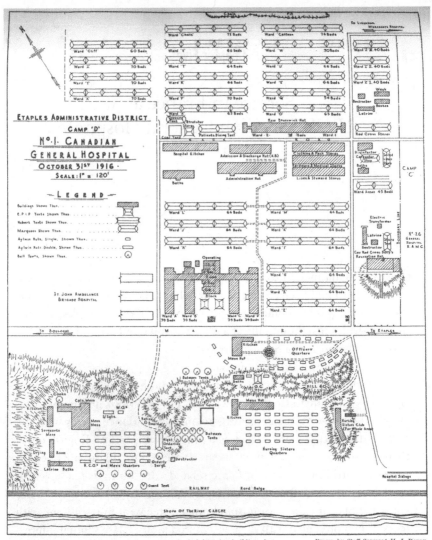

This Plan is based upon a drawing of the wards and administrative buildings but not including the living quarters made at the time to illustrate the distribution of beds by Sergeant-Major (W O 1) M. F. MILLARD, and expanded from information supplied by a number of the personnel of the hospital. Some of the tents and buildings may not be placed accurately nor drawn to scale.

Drawn by Staff-Sergeant H. J. Kenny, R.C.E. Chief draughtsman, M.D. No. 4.

No. 1 Canadian General Hospital. Cameron, p. 286

well on account of the wind which at times threatened to blow everything in the hut away as we had the ends open"; and later, "July 17. Very windy all day with rain at times."

It would be some time before No. 1 CGH could operate at full capacity of 1,040 beds. When it opened on May 31, fewer than half that number were set up, and construction of the tent wards for the patients continued for some time, all of which altered the staff's schedule. Clare's early days were "the usual routine of Surgical Supplies and bed making for me today as my ward is not ready yet." Her entry on May 28, 1915, records: "Our work is progressing, but it is so enormous that a day's work does not show for much. We have about 400 beds ready now." Within the next couple of days, Clare received her first patients: "When we arrived went on duty & received fifty-one patients, some badly, some only slightly wounded. Only two or three Canadians among them."

Hospitals in France were set up to receive all incoming wounded from the Allied forces, as well as civilians and prisoners of war. Naturally, the nurses were most anxious to care for their own countrymen, and Clare's diary notes whenever she encountered someone she knew. In one entry, Clare described her feelings at seeing the troop trains heading toward the front: "Troops go through on the trains (& such long trains) almost daily, with guns and gun carriages in sight. When we are able, we wave strenuously & they also. They seem so happy & full of life. Poor lads. There is a difference when they come back on the Ambulance trains: then it is usually night & they are silent, and we are too." By early July, Clare was noting that the process of evacuation of patients from France to England had begun: "July 6. I got fifteen new patients last night & sent out twelve of my old ones today to the Hospital ship & home to England."

Nursing sisters quickly learned the grim realities of their work. Within a week of the hospital's opening, Clare described her reaction to the incoming patients' "dreadful wounds. One young boy with part of his face shot away both arms gone & great wounds in both legs.... These are the horrors of war but they are too horrible. Can it be God's will or only man's devilishness.... Our boy with both arms gone is only twenty years old." By mid-June, the volume of cases at No. 1 CGH had increased. On

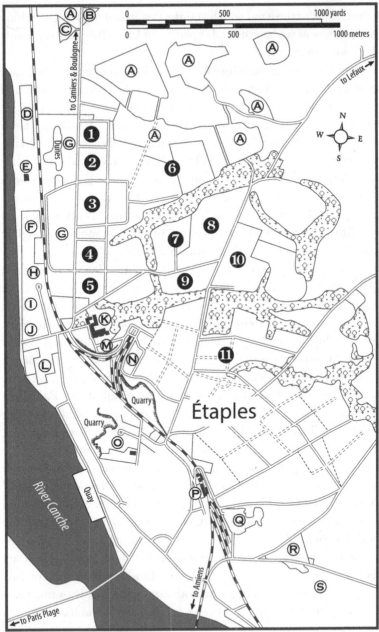

Mike Bechthold

June 17, Clare noted: "A convoy of 180 patients came in tonight. Very few Canadians.... We have received over 800 patients here in the last two weeks & we are only a tiny part of this great sea of hospital tents."

Both Clare and her colleague, Sophie Hoerner, had to care for patients with major trauma early in their service near the front. Their experience was very different from the cases Anna received during this same period at Moore Barracks. Later in June, Clare recorded her reaction to their injuries:

> A convoy of patients arrived this morning. Some terrible cases, oh so much better dead (one young lad with eyes & nose all gone — one blur of mangled flesh — & body whole & sound) heads shattered to pieces or limbs hanging by a thread of tendons. Oh why must such things be. All are so brave, & yet those who are not badly wounded are so tired of the war, at least those who have been long in the trenches — tired in such a hopeless way.

(opposite): Étaples Administrative District

1. St. John's Ambulance Brigade Hospital
2. No. 1 Canadian General Hospital
3. No. 26 General Hospital
4. No. 7 Canadian General Hospital / No. 23 General Hospital
5. No. 24 General Hospital
6. No. 51 General Hospital / Allied Forces Hospital
7. No. 51 General Hospital for Officers
8. No. 56 General Hospital
9. No. 46 Stationary Hospital / Isolation Hospital
10. No. 6 Convalescent Hospital
11. No. 18 General Hospital

A. No. 2 Training Camp
B. Mortuary
C. Cemetery
D. Segregation Camp
E. Portuguese Detention Compound
F. Detention Compound
G. Personnel of Hospitals
H. Royal Engineer Camp
I. Base Details
J. Laundry
K. Chateau
L. Headquarters
M. Royal Engineers
N. Army Service Corps
O. Women's Hostel
P. Train Station
Q. Motor Transport Pool
R. Horse Transport Pool
S. Quarry Rifle Range

Sophie had a similar reaction to her patients' wounds. On June 4, she wrote, "Oh dear, if you could see the dreadful smashups of these splendid fellows. It's awful and I cry many, many times. I can't get used to it. It's so dreadful." By the time Anna and her colleagues at Moore Barracks received these patients, they had already been triaged, treated, and sent on for recovery or additional surgeries. The time would come, however, when Anna, too, would face the melee of triage and intake.

The nursing staff took advantage of periods of relative calm to socialize with the staff of other hospitals in the area. The hospitals were about forty miles from the fighting and in close proximity to one another. On June 2, Clare noted that she walked "four miles in the heat and came back in the Ambulance" when she was invited to tea at No. 2 Stationary Hospital at Le Touquet. The nurses got a half-day off periodically, which, from her diary entries, was roughly once a week when the caseload permitted. Clare's diary notes a half-day off on June 3 and again on July 8 and July 14. A respite from the strain of care was essential, and Clare's diary records times with her colleagues, exploring the countryside, attending church services, and resting in their off hours to alleviate the stress. After purchasing bicycles from local residents, Clare describes how she and her comrades rode around the countryside in their off hours, including trips to Dannes-Camiers, a few miles up the coast toward Boulogne, where their hospital was being set up.

By July 1915, the pace of the fighting was accelerating, and on July 8, within a week of accepting patients, Clare noted in her diary: "am very tired at the end of the day just now. My ward is a busy one just now." On July 19, six weeks after first taking in patients at No. 1 CGH, Clare and her colleagues moved to their newly constructed hospital, No. 3 CGH (McGill). While waiting to provide patient care, Clare's anxiety and loneliness after two months' service in France is evident: "Last Post is just sounding. They are such sad notes & have such a lonely sound." At No. 3 CGH, housed once again in tents, Clare was clearly concerned about their capacity to withstand the elements: "It is so windy in this part of the country & storms come up so suddenly that the tents need to be very secure. Last night we went to bed with a beautiful cloudless moonlit sky & at twelve o'clock it was pouring the heaviest rain I have ever seen & blowing a hurricane; I had to get up and hammer some of the tent pegs in & tie down my flap securely."

Part of Clare's frustration at this time was actually the lack of work at No. 3 CGH: "August 6. I wish we could get some patients. It seems so dreadful to be idling when there is so much to be done, but apparently the ADMS does not want us to get patients till the water supply is ready." Finally, on August 10, she noted: "We had a big convoy of wounded at 12:45. The fighting along the lines near Ypres has been heavy lately & the men say very successful but so many wounded & such tired men. They are all so pleased to get into bed. These men came from Hooge."

No. 3 CGH operated at Dannes-Camiers for only a few months. The facilities of a tent hospital proved inadequate, exposed as they were to the elements on the coast of France. In early November, No. 3 CGH was ordered closed. The hospital's matron, Katherine MacLatchy, from Grand Pré, Nova Scotia, reported: "November 7, we received orders to close up, and the patients were evacuated to England. Some of the tents had blown down and the mud was almost impassable. The closing up and turning in of equipment occupied some time." By December, once all the equipment was packed up, Clare was transferred to England.

The hospital returned to France on January 3, 1916, setting up on the grounds of an old Jesuit College farther up the coast at Boulogne. Their new accommodation was a combination of huts made of galvanized iron, wood, and asbestos, a few tents, and part of the old college, which provided room for two thousand patients. Clare returned to France on February 14, and described the setting: "Such a beautiful situation. We have the old Jesuit College.... Our quarters (across the road, on the north of the medical huts in the field) are very comfortable."

Despite experiencing the same weather conditions as No. 3 CGH, No. 1 CGH remained in Étaples, working in tents for much of its service — the decision makers could not countenance closing two general hospitals at the same time. According to Kenneth Cameron, No. 1 CGH's historian, during one particular storm, "[e]ight unoccupied tents were blown down, the church tent, men's mess, mortuary, etc. while in the case of some others the ropes and pegs held but the canvas was torn to ribbons." During the storm, ninety-five stretcher cases were sent to England, but returned to No. 1 CGH when their boat was involved in an accident, before finally being sent back into the Channel once more.

The commanding officer at No. 1 CGH, Colonel Murray MacLaren, devoted much of his energy to improving the living and working conditions for the staff and patients under his care. When he and No. 1 CGH first arrived in France in May 1915, he met with Colonel H. Carr, ADMS, Étaples Administrative District, who pointed out to MacLaren that, within the EAD, "there were to be four camps to be occupied by hospital units, three to be equipped with huts and one with tents, and that No. 1 Canadian General Hospital was to have the tents." Despite MacLaren's protests that No. 1 CGH had spent months of suffering and hardship in England, the decision was made: No. 1 CGH would be established at Étaples as a tent hospital.

During 1915, MacLaren got approval to erect a hut to accommodate the sickest patients, built with funds donated by the people of New Brunswick. The New Brunswick Hut (Hut No. 1) opened on November 30, 1915, just as winter set in. Over each bed was a small shield bearing the name of the donor, and on the hut door was emblazoned the coat of arms of New Brunswick. The first patient to be admitted was Private L.E. Harrington (69432) of the 26th Battalion, from West Saint John. Two nursing sisters from Saint John, Mary L. Domville and Edith McCafferty, were put in charge of the wards.

The New Brunswick Hut accommodated fifty-eight patients in the two wards. It provided better facilities than tents for the worst-off patients, and included a service room, scullery, and two small rooms at the far end for a latrine and washroom. In a hospital set up for 1,040 beds, however, the hut could accommodate only about 5 percent of the soldier patients; the remainder were housed in tent wards for the winter of 1915-16. Not all hospitals remained tented. Katharine Wilson-Simmie described her

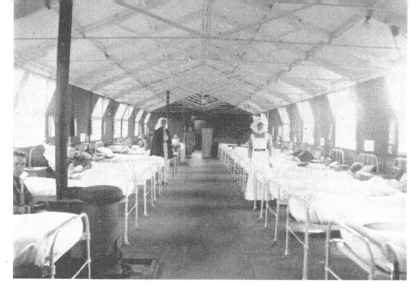

New Brunswick Hut, with Nursing Sisters Margaret Parks, M.D.,
and Mary Domville. Cameron, p. 229

New Brunswick Hut entrance. Cameron, p. 228

thoughts when she returned to No. 7 CSH in Étaples in 1917: "When I had been on duty in 1915, in Étaples, the hills now covered with wooden huts had been a city of canvas marquees. More and more the war and all branches of it seemed to have settled down into a systematic business, complete with conveniences."

In 1915, when the Western Front settled into trench warfare, continuous exposure to the wet and mud resulted in a new wave of diseases, including trench foot, which manifested itself in swelling, edema, and pain, "with not infrequently death of the part." The soldiers, who were expected to prevent it, were instructed to "wash their feet as thoroughly as possible, stimulate circulation by rubbing, grease them, and change their socks twice a day while in the trenches." According to Cameron, if a man failed to follow this regimen and showed signs of the disease, it was a punishable offence. Clearly, given the living and working conditions, this advice was difficult to follow. Trench foot continued as the war progressed. In February and March 1916, at No. 1 CGH, "there was an increase in the number of sick, a large proportion being due to trench-feet, trench fever and nephritis...this type of wounds [sic] continued to be severe during the latter part of March. The convoys were then coming from the sector held by the Canadian Corps." Cameron describes trench fever as "a condition characterized by fever, headache, pain in the back but especially in the legs, 'shin plains' and long irregular convalescence." Major Allen Rankin, one of No. 1 CGH's officers, authored an article in the *Lancet* in which this condition was described as "a new and definite pathological entity." As Cameron points out, trench fever continued to plague soldiers, since it was believed to be carried by lice, and persisted despite "active de-lousing treatments."

The volume of cases increased significantly in late 1915, with the caseload reaching a high of 1,993 patients in November. Much of the increase in admissions was for disease rather than for wounds, although this might have been a classification issue. The Germans had begun using chlorine gas in April 1915, and the effects on the soldiers was devastating: Morton notes that little could be done for them beyond giving them rest and oxygen. Later on, the Germans introduced phosgene, an odourless

A patient examines the helmet
that saved his life. Cameron, p. 277

and colourless gas that turned into
hydrochloric acid on contact with
moisture — such as inside lungs. In
a diary entry on May 2, 1916, while
at No. 3 CGH in Boulogne, Clare
Gass noted: "The gas cases of last
night tell me that the wind changed
suddenly on Sunday and before they
could move the gas was upon them.
It was sleeping hours and most of the
men had to be wakened. Many never
woke again." Morton notes that 11,536
Canadians were treated in hospital for the effects of chemicals.

By early 1916, there were fewer admissions for penetration wounds
as the impact of improvements in military equipment became evident.
During January, "among the wounded, though the smallest number
for any month, many were severe, there being an unusual proportion of
injuries to the head and chest." Most of these were caused by shrapnel
shells exploding over trenches, where men were otherwise reasonably
safe. By February and March, the military had finally decided to issue
steel helmets, which "soon proved their value," and the number of head
injuries declined significantly. "Those that were seen were not as severe
as formerly."

Anna Stamers arrived in France to begin her service at No. 1 CGH
on February 19, 1916. Her time at the hospital was the longest period
she spent at any location during her service. She was one of a group of
nine nursing sisters reassigned from Moore Barracks. Six members of
this group had sailed together from Montreal and worked together at
Shorncliffe. Whether the decision to move the women as a group was
deliberate or not, it no doubt facilitated their transition and allowed them

to support one another personally and professionally. Anna's two colleagues from the Saint John School of Nursing, Ethel Moody and Nellie Floyd, were part of the group and continued to serve with Anna for the next fifteen months. In addition to her two Saint John friends, another New Brunswick nurse, Irene Barton from Pine Ridge, Kent County, was part of the group initially assigned to Moore Barracks and transferred to No. 1 CGH with Anna that February.

Other nursing sisters from New Brunswick were already at No. 1 CGH when Anna arrived, including Dr. Margaret Parks, Mabelle Jamieson, Mary Domville, Edith McCafferty, Nellie Donohoe, and Nellie MacDonald. Anna would never again work with so many colleagues from her home province. She would need their support. While Anna worked at No. 1 CGH, the Canadian Corps fought three major battles: Mount Sorrel outside Ypres in June 1916, the Battle of the Somme in September-November 1916, and Vimy Ridge in April 1917. These were among the most significant Canadian battles of the First World War, and they resulted in huge numbers of wounded soldiers.

By the time Anna and her colleagues reached No. 1 CGH, the hospital had been operating in France for nine months and was a fully functioning tent hospital where procedures were already established. No. 1 CGH was a much larger facility and wounded were often taken directly there for care. Cameron says that it was a general hospital, but "in reality an enlarged, better equipped, more stable and supposedly safe Casualty Clearing Station. The pressure from the front meant that patients were quickly transferred to convalescence or back to duty." It had a larger nursing team caring for double the number of beds. It was double the size of Moore Barracks, which had a nursing complement of forty and was authorized for five hundred to eight hundred beds while Anna worked there.

For Anna and her colleagues, the biggest change would have been their location so much closer to the front, and at a more central point in the evacuation chain. Only after they were stabilized were patients moved by hospital ship to England and sent on to hospitals such as Moore Barracks. The other major change was that, in 1916, the pace of action at

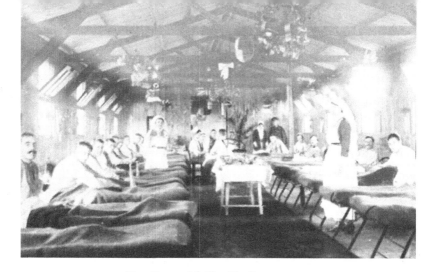

New Brunswick Hut No. 3. Cameron, p. 318

the front picked up dramatically. Nurses now had their hands full, instead of experiencing the frustrating idleness about which Laura Holland, Elsie Collis, and Clare Gass complained. The Canadian Corps was now big enough that, even during quiet periods, the flow of wounded was steady.

Anna's living and working environment at No. 1 CGH was no improvement over Moore Barracks. In his *War Story of the Canadian Army Medical Corps*, J. George Adami confirms that the New Brunswick Hut, No. 1 Hut, and the Administrative Block were the only huts erected for No. 1 CGH that first winter in France. "Save for these," Adami notes, "through gales and frost, No. 1 somehow pulled through the autumn and winter of 1915/16 in tents." Adami records that the officers and nursing sisters were housed in Alwyn huts, which he describes as "small, detached cubicle apartments of light wooden framework, ten by twelve, with canvas stretched over wooden floors and celluloid windows." Adami assures his readers that, despite the huts' rudimentary structure, "they were more comfortable than the description implies, and they were retained after the patients transferred to hutments." No. 1 CGH also constructed mess huts such that, by early January, "the officers, nursing sisters, the sergeants and the men experienced the comfort of having a weather-proof roof over their heads while having their meals."

Despite changes to the tents, a Court of Inquiry was held on February 25, 1916, to investigate the serviceability of the tent wards. Cameron notes that this did not result in any change, as "apparently it did not condemn the use of tents for a hospital situated as No. 1 was on the exposed sand dunes and subject to the lashings by the westerly gales off the sea." Thereafter, the leadership of No. 1 CGH put their efforts into building more huts. Further funds from New Brunswick supplied the resources required to construct an Admission and Discharge Hut, which opened at the end of August. Another hut ward for patients, New Brunswick Hut No. 3, opened on June 15, 1917. Anna, then, lived in an Alwyn hut, and spent most of her working hours in tents. Perhaps, from time to time, she and her colleagues were afforded the opportunity to work in the New Brunswick Hut No. 1 or the Admission and Discharge Hut.

After Anna left No. 1 CGH in May 1917, work continued on another hut, New Brunswick Hut, Ward No. 3. When completed, a plaque with the names of the New Brunswick donors was installed. Cameron, p. 318

By the time Anna arrived, the weather had already taken a nasty turn. Initially, 1916 was unseasonably warm, and the bushes had begun to bloom when the temperature rose to 16 degrees Celsius. But less than a week after her arrival, on February 24, "the thermometer suddenly took [a] drop to 20 degrees [-7 degrees Celsius] and a heavy snowstorm raged for three days." Anna worked in tents heated by coal-fired stoves. Water pipes were installed along the outside and, as a fire-prevention measure, water pails were kept inside the tents. During the winters of 1916 and 1917, the water in the outside pipes and in the pails inside the tents froze. Snow on the tent roofs had to be removed to prevent collapse, and paths were cleared between the tents to allow access to the patients. In March, the weather was not as cold, but on March 29 the wind was heavy enough to rip some of the tents and take the roof off several others. This was Anna's experience of military nursing in winter on the sand dunes of France. The working conditions in the winter months of January to March 1917 were brutal. Cameron notes:

> The French newspapers reported that the severity of the winter had broken all records since 1885. It had been a season of great hardship for all in the hospital, not so much for the patients, for the supply of blankets was plentiful and their sojourn was short, but to the attendants, especially the nursing sisters, who went about their duties without a murmur, ever cheerful, while suffering severely from the cold during the long days and longer nights.

The nurses worked twelve-hour shifts, and after five to seven days had a half-day off. The realities of war, however, did not always permit adherence to schedules, and even when nurses had worked a full daytime shift, they could not count on a full night's sleep. Convoys came at night because the wounded were removed from the battlefield only under cover of darkness. As volumes increased, nurses who were scheduled to work in the daytime might well have had to help with the intake when the convoys arrived.

When Anna began working at No. 1 CGH in mid-February 1916, patients were staying in the hospital for an average of eight to twelve days. Consequently, from the outset, Anna had the opportunity to get to know her patients, as she would have had them in her care for a week or more. By March 1916, the caseload increased to 1,657 soldiers, more than double the number admitted in January; of these, 580 were wounded, the rest sick. Despite Anna's hard introduction to No. 1 CGH because of the weather, the demands from incoming wounded remained relatively light that spring. According to Cameron, "April, at the Front, had been regarded as a fairly quiet month, and during May the only major activity along the whole line was in the Ypres sector where the Canadian divisions were stationed." The medical cases, at 727, still outnumbered those wounded, with a noted increase in cases of trench fever and nephritis. Of the 619 cases admitted with wounds, most were due to lacerations from shrapnel, resulting in 292 operations. In the first few months, Anna was part of a bigger team, in a larger hospital, but still dealing with a larger proportion of sick than wounded soldiers. That was to drastically change in the summer of 1916 with the opening of the Battle of the Somme.

The leadership of No. 1 CGH recognized that the medical staff needed some respite from the suffering. They also needed to pause and commemorate those whose service had ended in death. Social activities, visits from dignitaries, and religious services provided some recognition of their efforts and consolation in their losses. In March 1916, Major-General J.M. Simms, CMG, Principal Chaplain to the Forces, toured the hospital. Easter Sunday, April 12, 1916, was set aside as a day of quiet reflection and commemoration. As Cameron describes it, "[t]he church tent, beautifully decorated with flowers, was filled to capacity at all the services." That same day, the staff took the time to commemorate those who had died: at 5:00 a.m., "a group of nursing sisters from No. 1 CGH led by Matron Nesbitt and Nursing Sisters Domville and MacInnes and detachments from other hospitals proceeded to the cemetery and laid flowers upon the graves."

However, any respite or consolation that these services might have afforded Anna and her colleagues was not to last. Just two days later,

Incendiary bomb dropped on No. 1
Canadian Hospital the night of
April 25/26, 1916. Cameron, p. 243

at midnight on April 25/26, German
Zeppelin No. 14 released two bombs
on No. 1 CGH. The target might have
been a mobilization and reinforcement camp about one mile southeast
of the hospital, but the bombs dropped
directly on the hospital. Clare Gass,
serving nearby at No. 3 CGH, now in
Boulogne, noted the incident in her
diary: "April 26 Last night there was an air raid at Étaples which is now a
big base for troops. Several incendiary bombs were dropped near 24 Gen
H and No. 1 Cdn but fortunately did no harm." Anna had been subjected
to the threat of bombs from Zeppelins earlier at Moore Barracks, so, although the incident was no doubt alarming, it was not new. As was the
case at Moore Barracks, the proximity of the hospital to the reinforcement
camp for soldiers was the real issue.

In contrast to the austere atmosphere at Moore Barracks, the leadership of No. 1 CGH involved the staff and patients in social activities,
which provided some respite from the stresses of war. A large hut, known
as the Canadian Red Cross recreation hut, was erected as a theatre and
concert hall "for the entertainment of all ranks in the Étaples district,"
and the officers had a club in the home of "one of the well-known art-
ists of Étaples." A group of non-commissioned officers and men started
a minstrel group, and Cameron says, with their "musical and histrionic
talent," they entertained the patients in the afternoon and the officers and
nursing sisters in the evening. The officers of No. 1 CGH regularly entertained guests, and a weekly guest night became routine. This included
social mixing between the male medical staff and the nursing sisters; as
the Canadian nursing sisters held the rank of lieutenant, this facilitated

more of such interaction. Cameron notes that, starting in 1915, tea in the nursing sisters' mess became an established social function.

These social events were so important to morale that they continued despite incoming convoys of wounded. No. 1 CGH had organized a sports field day for May 1, 1916, to celebrate May Day. Just the night before, 180 patients, the largest convoy in more than three weeks, arrived. Nonetheless, Cameron reports, "all were settled in before 2:30 p.m. after which the sports event started." Officers, nursing sisters, and other ranks from the different hospitals and adjoining camps came to participate or watch, with music provided by the Salvation Army band. Cameron describes the colourful scene: "The varied uniforms of the nursing sisters with their flowing veils, the gray and scarlet of the British and the Australians, the blue of the Canadians, the black, gray and white of the St. John Ambulance, the green of the Liverpool Merchants, the Khaki of the Americans, with the hospital blues of the patients and the khaki of the troops, all blended harmoniously with the green foliage of the pine trees." Cameron attributes the collegiality to Colonel MacLaren, who set the tone at No. 1 CGH. According to Cameron, what differentiated No. 1 CGH from the other hospitals in the district was "the esprit de corps that existed among the ranks, especially in that original group of experienced non-commissioned officers and men, the untiring devotion to duty of the nursing sisters, and the professional administrative efficiency which characterized the work of the officers."

It was at this same May Day celebration that No. 1 CGH had its first change of command after Colonel MacLaren was promoted to Deputy Director of Medical Services (DMS), Canadian Contingents, at CAMC Headquarters in London. Anna, Ethel, and Nellie had worked under his leadership for just two and a half months. Still, it must have been a proud moment for his fellow Saint John residents. In its first year of operation, No. 1 CGH admitted 16,582 patients. Of those, 7,151 were admitted as wounded and the remainder due to sickness. Cameron says that, by this time, No. 1 CGH "had lost its original connections and had no affiliation with any militia, university or other organization, city or province."

On May 11, Colonel Charles F. Wylde replaced MacLaren as commanding officer at No. 1 CGH. The hospital's time under Colonel Wylde's leadership, as Cameron notes, would be "its busiest and trying period for patient care, the early summer of 1916 until the fall of 1917." No. 1 CGH expanded to cope, but quickly reached its capacity to take patients. Later, when Colonel Wylde was also transferred, it was said that, during his tenure, "no patient was every refused admission and that the staff of the DDMS, EAD, knew that, however pressed they were for space, they could always rely upon 'No. 1 Can.' to find the beds." Two especially busy periods were from July to November 1916 during the Battle of the Somme and the Battle of Vimy Ridge in April 1917, when Anna and her Saint John colleagues served at No. 1 CGH under the strain of huge caseloads and the highest turnover of patients. For Anna, it was the most demanding caseload she would experience during her service.

Proximity to the front meant that the wounded typically arrived on the stretcher that carried them off the battlefield still wearing mud-caked clothes and dirty bandages. An orderly working with Anna would remove the soldiers' clothes and ensure that they were somewhat clean before she took over. Stephen McGreal writes: "For centuries the French farmers boosted the fertility of their soil by the use of animal manure as a fertilizer. This highly fertile soil contained the tetanus (lockjaw) virus and gaseous gangrene germs which soon infected wounds received upon the battlefield." Anna's role was to clean, disinfect, and bandage these wounds. During 1915, No. 1 CGH was the first to practise the Carrel-Dakin method, an irrigation process for treating wounds. Multiple perforated tubes were inserted into the wounds, which were bathed with an antiseptic solution to keep infection down. Bandages, which nurses changed regularly, kept the tubes in place. As Toman describes, the process "was devised solely and entirely for the purpose of enabling it thoroughly to saturate and bathe repeatedly every part of the wound with the solution." The practice became so common at No. 1 CGH that, in 1917, an entire ward was devoted to patients being cared for this way. Desmond Morton's quotation from Sergeant Thomas Geggie best illustrates the challenge the method posed for both the nurse and the patient during the twice-daily ceremony of "changing the plugs":

The withdrawal of the plugs caused me to emit my first, and only, hospital yell. It was a good yell, though perhaps I say it who shouldn't. I was immediately told it was a most ungentlemanly thing to do: that as an old soldier and a non-commissioned officer of some standing, I ought to show a better example. From that day, I resorted to the time-honored expedient of chewing holes in my leather belt during the plugging and unplugging.

The management of wounds was critical, since no antibiotics then existed. Doctors cut away infected or damaged flesh, a process called debridement, which, although drastic, saved the lives of many. Nurses administered oxygen and medications. Although Anna would have taken temperatures and recorded vital signs many times before at Moore Barracks, the challenge of monitoring patients suffering from gas gangrene and major wounds at No. 1 CGH was significantly different. Morton notes that the constant strain of suffering and death took a toll on the nursing sisters: "Once they completed their surgery or assigned a treatment, doctors could dismiss their patients but nurses carried on caring for men puffed to double their size with gangrene, stinking beyond a stomach's tolerance and suffering unspeakable agony."

In June, after three and a half months at No. 1 CGH, Anna became ill. Between her hospitalization and convalescence, Anna was off sick for twenty days with an ear infection. She recovered, and rejoined her unit on June 28. Many of the nursing sisters experienced multiple bouts of illness and periods of hospitalization. Like Anna, they were cared for at No. 24 CGH, set up in the residence of a Romanian nobleman and also known as the Villa Tino. According to her service file, this was the only occasion Anna was hospitalized during her entire period of service at No. 1 CGH. In fact, her file does not contain a medical report on her hospitalization, and this is the only reference to her illness. Living in such rudimentary facilities during the late winter and early spring took its toll on others as well. Cameron reports that, in the first quarter of 1916, "there was an undue amount of sickness with one nursing sister admitted to the hospital with pneumonia."

Fortunately for her colleagues, during Anna's absence the caseload had been "extremely light." For the whole month of June, there were 1,345 admissions, of which 708 were for wounds. Cameron reports that "[t]wo large convoys arrived—214 on June 4 and 381 on June 8. From June 9 to 21 no patients were admitted and on June 21 only 133 patients remained in the wards." It proved to be a period of relative respite for the staff of No. 1 CGH. During the last ten days of June, before Anna returned to duty, the hospital received another 700 patients, some of whom, as Cameron reports, were suffering from "recent wounds and severe illness [while] the majority seemed to be the clearing of the casualty clearing stations." Cameron does not specify, but the incoming wounded might have been from the Battle of Mount Sorrel (Hill 62) in the Ypres Salient, which had raged from June 2 to June 13.

Anna returned to her unit on Dominion Day, July 1, 1916. It was just as well that Anna had recovered by then, since the pace of work and demands suddenly increased dramatically. The devastation of the Battle of the Somme was about to test the three Canadian general hospitals in France: No. 1 CGH at Étaples, No. 3 CGH at Boulogne, and No. 2 CGH at Le Tréport. As Cameron notes, by the end of June, "[i]t became evident that preparations for an attack on a great scale were in progress, troop and ammunition trains were passing constantly in a southerly direction and orders had been received from D.D.M.S. E.A.D. to clear the hospital as far as possible." On July 2, Clare Gass noted in her diary: "We are making preparations for a great rush & all leave has been cancelled." During the months ahead, the staff at No.1 CGH would need to call upon the legacy and esprit de corps that Colonel MacLaren had established.

Despite the rumours of demands to come, the staff held a memorial service on Dominion Day, which Colonel Wylde described as both a fit and appropriate way of "doing honour to Canada's dead heroes on Canada's natal day." The parade of the nursing sisters, headed by Matron V.C. Nesbitt, was both dramatic and impressive, as Cameron describes:

[T]he men were arrested by the touch of colour that their uniforms lent to the scene and occasion. The light blue uniforms, dark blue capes and white veils were first noticeable, then as the capes swung open with the movements of the wearers a lining of vivid red was revealed. In their hands the nursing sisters carried bunches of flowers and as they passed between the ranks to take up their position in the centre of the parade there was none but whose heart swelled with pride for their Canadian women and the unspoken words were "God Bless them."

That evening, the officers and nursing sisters organized a concert. Cameron notes: "The sisters' part was exceptionally good, Nursing Sister Barton's Irish songs were much appreciated as was Nursing Sisters Howard and Barton's Irish jig." Before the night was over, however, a convoy of seventy-nine patients from the Ypres sector arrived, and seventy-seven were evacuated to England.

The next day, Sunday, July 2, began with two church services, but the tranquillity of the services was overtaken by rumours of a great battle in progress. While No. 1 CGH was honouring Dominion Day, the British Expeditionary Force (BEF) launched its largest offensive of the war to date. On July 1, the first day of the attack, the BEF suffered catastrophic casualties, losing nearly 60,000 troops by noon. The tidal wave of wounded men swamped the medical system. The first convoy of 393 arrived at No. 1 CGH at 2:15 p.m., followed by a second. In the early hours of July 3, 500 men arrived direct from the clearing stations at the front, while a convoy of 107 was dispatched to England. Instructions then were received to add another six hundred beds; the challenge was where to set them up. Cameron explains how they managed:

The Canadian Red Cross Society's recreation hut, with its wide verandah enclosed by canvas, afforded room for one hundred beds, the stage was fitted up as a surgical dressing room, and the barber shop as a service room, the church tents were converted into wards, and in the established wards, beds were placed close together after the stove bases had been removed. It was then necessary to erect a number of marquees. This logistical challenge was addressed, and the space adapted in time to accept the incoming wounded with the help of fifty Australian troops stationed in the district who came "armed with picks, shovels and saws, to render every possible assistance."

Demands from the front grew even greater. An order was received for six nurses to proceed immediately to the front to assist at the casualty clearing stations, which left only a supervisor and fourteen nursing sisters on night duty to handle the incoming wounded. Cameron describes the difficulty: "On the days and nights of July 4 to 8, convoy followed convoy. The cases then arriving had more serious wounds and the majority were on stretchers. An order was received that congestion of the lines of evacuation must be avoided and everyone who could possibly be moved should be sent to England without delay, consequently large discharge convoys were being dispatched between those which were arriving from the Front."

There was little time to make all these changes and be ready to accept the incoming wounded. The nursing sisters had to rearrange the beds, get the mobile ready to move, while assessing and caring for the incoming wounded. The system of hospitals in France was overwhelmed, and some men recovered from the battlefield were not taken off their stretchers and cleaned until they reached Edinburgh, in Scotland, many days later. Cameron records: "During that first week of July until the great influx of wounded men lessened there were 1909 admitted and 1543 discharged, the majority to England." By the end of July, No. 1 CGH had handled 4,363 admissions, almost three times as many as during any previous month since it opened, of which 3,808 were as a result of wounds and 555 from disease. The average number of days per patient was 4.37; there was little time for Anna and her colleagues to connect with their patients.

The nature of wounds treated at No. 1 CGH in July 1916 was such

New Brunswick Admission and Discharge Hut. Cameron, p. 279

that only 110 soldiers were returned to duty that month. The majority were sent to the Convalescent Depot (1,112) or evacuated to England (2,419). Despite the volume of cases and the challenge of providing care, only 51 soldiers died at No. 1 CGH that month. Morton states that a soldier who made it to a general hospital had a good chance of survival, while triage close to the battlefield meant that only those with a reasonable probability of recovery were sent to hospitals. "British statistics, based on a large sample of wounded, showed that 7 percent of wounded died at the [Regimental Aid Post or Advanced Dressing Station] and 16 percent at the CCS, where triage formally segregated both minor and hopeless cases and left the latter to be sedated and nursed, if possible, until their inevitable deaths."

During the four months of the Somme campaign, the 12,700 wounded admitted to No. 1 CGH demanded an unbelievable amount of effort on the part of every individual in the hospital and the expenditure of an enormous quantity of material—Cameron writes that, during the busiest periods, the hospital used an average of one mile of surgical gauze each day, which the nursing sisters had to prepare during their off hours. There was some relief when eight nursing sisters arrived from England, and before the end of July the recreation hut was restored to its normal use.

Although, as Cameron records, "[t]here had been no time, opportunity or desire for organized entertainment."

As a result of the experience of handling the deluge of patients during the Battle of the Somme, the decision was made to build an Admission and Discharge Hut. By the end of August, the hut, named "The New Brunswick Admission and Discharge Hut," was ready. The New Brunswick coat of arms was placed over the entrance and plaques bearing the names of subscribers suitably hung. This was the second wooden hut built at No. 1 CGH using funds provided by New Brunswick donors.

By September, as Andrew Macphail relates, "the Battle of the Somme had entered upon the third month of the most desperate fighting when on September 1 the Canadian Corps arrived there from the then comparatively quiet sector about Ypres and the struggle continued with increasing fury for the next two months." For Canadian soldiers, the battle opened on September 3 and lasted until November 28, during which time 1st, 2nd, and 3rd Canadian Divisions had 13,400 wounded; in mid-October, 4th Division had another 3,059. This was in addition to the devastating losses of Newfoundlanders at the Somme. Cameron says this period tested the capacity and the endurance of No. 1 CGH's personnel for "work and ever more work that must be undertaken." Daily convoys ranged from 150 to over 600 wounded men, but admissions were handled "expeditiously and systematically in the newly constructed" New Brunswick Admission and Discharge Hut. On September 19, the staff coped with 1,618 admissions in one day—almost as many as had been admitted in the entire month of September the previous year. As Table 1 shows, the numbers did not begin to trend downwards until the early winter of 1917.

Table 1.

Patients Received at No. 1 Canadian General Hospital, July-December 1916

	July	August	September	October	November	December
Total	4,363	2,768	4,756	4,875	3,058	2,195
Wounded	3,808	1,980	3,785	3,193	936	276
Sick	555	788	965	1,682	2,122	1,919

At the height of the Battle of the Somme, the administrative skills of hospital staff were needed to make space for incoming wounded. During the summer and fall, there were two periods of intense admissions. After the first intake in July, the district administrators arranged that No. 1 CGH should take admissions only on alternate days for a ten-day period. As Cameron notes, "[i]n that way the district headquarters administration gave the personnel an opportunity to obtain the needed rest and renewal of their vigour and for the hospital to resume a more normal condition." In her diary during this period, Clare Gass recorded instances when admissions would alternate between No. 1 CGH and No. 3 CGH to spread the workload.

During the Somme campaign, the nursing sisters sustained a pace that was almost more than they could endure. There was no time for socializing, and the staff had to call on that esprit de corps for which No. 1 CGH was noted. According to Cameron, "[t]here was but one thought in the minds of all in the hospital and that was work and ever more work that must be undertaken. There was no time to think of anything else such as the reception of visitors and entertainments were not considered except for the few concerts provided by the local regimental bands." Morton quotes Elizabeth Paynter, a nursing sister who served at No. 1 CGH during this period and, on a particularly difficult night during the Somme offensive, recorded her thoughts:

> A haemorrhage, emergency operation, followed by an intravenous saline and constant watching and treatment until 3 a.m. when the fine-looking New Zealand boy quietly breathed his last. The same night another patient died, and another still was very low, while there were at least four other delirious head cases, who seemed to take turns pulling off their dressings or getting out of bed. We also had a number of gas gangrene cases, and these are quite a worry, as the infection travels so fast, and last, but not least, the haemorrhages which so often occur in the dead of night when the lights are dim. Here is where my flashlight served

me in good stead and I then blessed old matron for insisting on us buying them in Kingston, where we were outfitted.

No. 1 CGH had some changes in staffing during this time, as the pace clearly took its toll on some members. During September and October, sixteen nursing sisters reported for duty, while, of the existing staff, four were invalided to England, two were recalled to England for duty, and two were transferred to CCCS in France. So, during this busy time, the staff complement increased by only eight nurses.

With all the pressure to provide care to the wounded, the menace of weather again made life miserable. In November, No. 1 CGH was hit with a "terrific wind and rainstorm which blew down several tents," and in the next month "a notably severe storm struck the area at Christmas time when much damage was done." Colonel Wylde wrote strong protests to the DDMS Étaples Administrative District about the prospects of a severe winter and the unsuitability of the tents, but no action was taken. Perhaps the fact that No. 1 CGH had taken the initiative to erect two semi-permanent buildings made the prospect of closing it less urgent. Wylde's warnings about the weather proved prescient when, on December 23, a gale blew down two wards and the Canadian Red Cross supply tent and ripped the flies on twenty-one other tents beyond repair. Cameron states that, because of the danger of fire, every available person, including the nurses, guarded the tents at night, "and they as well as the patients suffered very much from the cold." In January and February, when Alice Isaacson was working in nearby Le Tréport, she complained: "such awfully cold weather. We simply perish while dressing in the morning. I'd rather go on duty hungry, than eat in our cold mess room." Later, she noted: "We are allowed to burn only two electric lights in a ward—the power plant is not sufficient to supply the hospital wards."

Despite the punishing workload of the previous six months, the inadequacies of the living conditions, and the vagaries of the weather, Christmas Day 1916 did not pass without celebration. According to Cameron, "[e]very effort was made to give the patients, of whom there were 1031 a pleasant day." The officers dressed up "in all sorts of ridicu-

Nursing Sister Edith McCafferty and her Christmas Eve Concert Party, 1916.

Cameron, p. 285

lous garments and with weird instruments procured in Paris marched through all the wards much to the delight of the onlookers." By year's end, No. 1 CGH had cared for 29,332 patients in 1916, of whom 16,758 were wounded (and 229 died) and 12,574 were ill from disease (and 22 died). At the end of 1916, seventy-nine nursing sisters were on the Nominal Roll at No. 1 CGH; of these, only six had served continuously since May 31, 1915, when the hospital opened.

At nearby No. 3 CGH, Clare Gass made two poignant entries in her diary as the year drew to a close. "Dec. 25. Peace on Earth and the world at war. Yet in spite of this fact we had such a happy, happy day doing for these lads, our best to make it a Happy Christmas…one of the happiest days I have ever spent." Then, on the last day of 1916, Clare wrote: "Dec. 31. Another year ended — a year filled with many sad yet many happy days — In our work in the Hospital we have been happy — the busy days full of interest — so busy that they have flown and the year on looking back has not been a long one in many ways — Yet when one looks at its toll of lives lost then it has been long indeed. Surely this coming year will bring peace to the world."

In January 1917, the nursing sisters at No. 1 CGH were finally given leave. Anna took hers on January 12, and rejoined the unit on January 25. Apart from half-days, this was her first extended leave since arriving in France almost a year previously and her first opportunity truly to relax and spend time away from the hospital. Anna's file simply records the fact and duration of her leave, but nothing else. According to Matron McCarthy, Matron-in-Chief, British Troops in France and Flanders, Canadian nursing sisters typically took their leave in the south of France, Italy, or most often in England. Clare spent her holiday in England with her brother. Ethel and Nellie took leave during the same period but just before Anna. Jean Templeman's and Anna's leaves coincided two weeks later, and, although there is no formal record of where they went, no doubt these friends spent their time together.

It had been an eventful eighteen months. Anna had spent Christmas 1915 and 1916 overseas, and on January 18, 1917, while on leave, celebrated her twenty-ninth birthday. No doubt she shared the occasion with her friends. Dr. Margaret Parks and Mary Domville, two of the senior nursing sisters who took leave in December 1916, travelled home to Saint John. The local newspaper account of their exploits was upbeat about the work of the nursing sisters at the front. Nothing in their comments would have given any reader any idea of the pressures they were under. Indeed, when Anna returned from leave near the end of January, the workload was still heavy. That month, the hospital received 2,572 cases, 1,493 in February and 2,933 in March.

Leave, however, had given Anna and her friends time to refresh and regroup. It was needed. When springtime came in 1917, everyone knew that another big offensive was looming: it was all over the French newspapers. Clare Gass noted in her diary on March 12: "Orders to clear the hospital in preparation for some special action. Rumour says Canadian casualties in the 4th division have been very heavy and that a big convoy of Canadians have come to Étaples. We have heard of none in Boulogne."

Following the experience of the Battle of the Somme, medical preparations improved in advance of the commencement of the Battle of Arras. The hospitals were asked to prepare estimates of their ability to expand

and to clear patients to England at the rate of 5,000 per day. Cameron notes that they completed their estimates on April 5, and 2,230 beds were ready for occupation. In addition, No. 1 CGH established two teams for Admissions and Discharge so that they did duty on alternate nights and could get rest. Nonetheless, by April 6, before the offensive began, 1,885 beds were already occupied.

The Battle of Arras, of which the Canadian attack on Vimy Ridge was a part, commenced on April 9. This most intense push for the Canadians lasted until April 12, but continuing attacks by British formations to the east of Vimy produced a huge number of additional casualties. During the four days of the Battle of Vimy Ridge, there were 6,971 admissions to No. 1 CGH alone. Again, Cameron's statistics tell the story best. The caseload in April 1917 was the highest for any month that No. 1 CGH would ever experience. Of these, 4,293 were wounded and 2,678 were sick. Figures for the next two months were still high at 3,284 in May and 4,255 in June, as the BEF fought on.

During this period, Anna discovered that she knew someone from New Brunswick who was wounded at Vimy Ridge: Lieutenant Stanley MacDonald, from Moncton. Despite the demands of her schedule, Anna made time to visit Lieutenant MacDonald, who was recovering in a nearby hospital. On May 8, the *Moncton Transcript* reported that he would return home to recuperate from his wounds. As a result of the wound he sustained at Vimy Ridge, Stanley had no use in his right hand, so Anna wrote to his family for him. She noted, "we are working every minute of the day, handling patients by the thousands." Stanley returned to Canada following the war, and in 1920 he married Anna's younger sister, Willa.

The physical and emotional toll these demands placed on the nursing sisters was wearing. Christine Hallett quotes from the diary of an Australian nurse, Elsie May Tranter, who was also based nearby in Étaples: "Today I had to assist on ten amputations one after another. It is frightfully nerve-wracking work. I seem to hear that wretched saw at work whenever I sleep. We see most ghastly wounds — and are all day long inhaling the odour of gas gangrene. How these boys do suffer! This war is absolute hell. We see and hear all day and every day the results of its frightfulness. We can hear the guns quite plainly here." As Hallett concludes, "[nursing work in the First World War was a dangerous pursuit.... [M]ost were able to withstand such experiences for a limited time... and some drove themselves beyond the limits of their endurance."

Wisely, by then, the matrons decided the nursing sisters needed a change. On May 17, Anna was transferred back to the CAMC Depot at Shorncliffe, England. Although, at No. 1 CGH, she had had the benefit of a well-established hospital and a well-functioning team of nursing sister colleagues, it had been a particularly difficult time. The cold weather and the inadequate housing made her living and working conditions the worst that she would experience. As a nurse, however, the greatest difficulty was the combined effect of high caseload volumes and patients with traumatic injuries. Sometimes, little could be done, and there was so little time to spend with any of the soldiers in those busiest of days. The sustained pace required of the nursing sisters from July to December 1916 and again in April and May 1917 tested Anna's endurance, as it no doubt did the endurance of all who were serving their country.

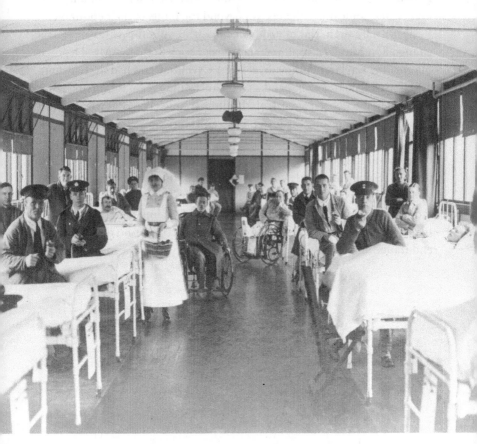

Ontario Military Hospital, Orpington, Kent,
later renamed No. 16 Canadian General Hospital, ca. 1916-17.

Ontario Military Hospital photographs, F 4386, Archives of Ontario, I0007454

Chapter Six

On the Move:
England, Canada, and England Again

Anna Stamers left No. 1 CGH on May 21, 1917, after fifteen months of continuous service in France. She never returned to the Western Front. Her time at No. 1 CGH proved to be her most onerous service, in terms of both duration and the pressure of high caseloads. No doubt, by the spring of 1917, she was weary in body and spirit. According to Kenneth Cameron, April 1917, during the Battle of Arras, was the most demanding period in the history of No. 1 CGH. But he also noted that May brought a period of calm to the hospital after the "extreme activity of April," and the administration took this opportunity to make changes in staffing.

In May, the nursing team was both increased and refreshed. Overall strength grew from seventy-two to one hundred, and nine nursing sisters were transferred out of No. 1 CGH. Of those, only two remained in France to serve at a casualty clearing station, one was invalided to England, two were admitted to hospital with diphtheria, and one, already on leave in England, was retained there. Anna, her colleague, Jean Templeman, and one other were sent back to England. Anna and Jean had sailed together to England, and then served together at Moore Barracks and again at No. 1 CGH. During the Battle of the Somme, Jean had served briefly at a casualty clearing station closer to the front. Nellie Floyd and Ethel Moody, Anna's colleagues from Saint John, stayed on at

No. 1 CGH, but shortly thereafter went on medical leave. Ethel never recovered sufficiently to serve again. Clearly, the strain of service at the front for such an extended period had taken its toll.

In his history of No. 1 CGH, Cameron records that, on May 21, Anna was assigned to duty on a hospital ship, but this assignment was later changed. According to her service file, Anna was posted to the CAMC Depot in Shorncliffe on May 21. On May 28, she was transferred to the Ontario Military Hospital, Orpington, Kent. During her short interval in Shorncliffe, she had another unnerving experience. On Friday, May 25, the Germans dropped multiple bombs on the unsuspecting population of Folkestone and the nearby military camp. The raid killed ninety-seven people, mostly civilians. Eighteen Canadian soldiers at Moore Barracks also died in the bombing.

Three days after the bombing, Anna was officially transferred to No. 16 CGH, Orpington. Then, on June 7, she was transferred back to the CAMC Depot. Her service file provides no explanation, but perhaps when Anna got to No. 16 CGH, Orpington, just after the bombing, the matron realized that she needed an extended break. Within two days of her transfer back to the CAMC Depot, she was granted a long leave. According to Jean Templeman's service file, she and Anna left for Canada on June 9 on the ocean liner SS *Scandinavian*. Jean's Militia and Defence file includes a letter dated June 18, stating: "a cable has been received from England reporting that arrangements had been made for the marginally noted nursing sister to sail from Liverpool to Canada on the 9th instant, SS *Scandinavian*. The above information is sent to you to advise you of her probable arrival in Canada at an early date. As it sometimes occurs that the departure of vessels for Canada is postponed for a few days her non-arrival at the time she is expected need not cause you any anxiety on her behalf." The ship's manifest records that SS *Scandinavian* did, in fact, depart Liverpool a day late, and arrived in Quebec on June 21 after a voyage of twelve days, port to port.

The crossing proved uneventful, although the trip was not likely a serene one. Even in 1915, when Anna and Jean first sailed from Canada to England, the risk of being torpedoed by a German submarine was a reality. The situation in 1917 was very much worse. The Germans made several attempts to launch unrestricted attacks on Allied shipping, only to have diplomatic pressure from neutrals force them to stop. Finally, in February 1917, the Germans threw caution to the wind and declared that they would not stop sinking shipping until they drove Great Britain to surrender. Losses to Allied shipping spiked that spring, but the U-boat campaign led the United States to declare war on Germany. Among the early casualties of this campaign were six hospital ships, all sunk in contravention of international law—the crossing on the *Scandinavian* had been more perilous than Anna and Jean could have known.

Upon arrival in Canada, Anna and Jean were authorized to take seventeen days' leave. This was much more generous than nursing sisters' typical ten-day leave every six months, schedules permitting. Presumably, since both Anna and Jean had endured a long period of service in France before being transferred to England and then a lengthy stay on a troopship while en route to Canada, they were granted a more generous period of leave. In fact, Anna spent nearly four months in Canada before returning to No. 16 CGH in the fall of 1917.

Anna and Jean seem to have taken the train to New Brunswick on June 22, as on June 23 the Saint John *Standard* reported that Anna had arrived home the previous day. Local people were interested in any news of the war, especially from someone returning from the front. The New Brunswick dailies reported their stories: when they were first taken on strength, when they left their home province to enlist, when they sailed, when they arrived, where they served, and any formal recognition they received as a result of their service. Nursing sisters on leave in Canada were treated like celebrities. Even though many of these women were not trained in public speaking, they often spoke at specially organized events. Local groups sponsored talks that newspapers across the province covered, even when the nursing sisters were not from the same community. The Imperial Order Daughters of the Empire (IODE), the Red Cross, and the nurses' associations were all interested in where these nursing sisters were serving and what they could tell them about how local initiatives were helping the war effort. Although the families of the soldiers and nursing sisters received letters and telegrams, the opportunity to hear the nursing sisters' experiences first-hand was likely very meaningful to those with sons and other relatives fighting in France. It was also a way of paying tribute to the young women who were providing medical care to their kin.

Not all stories were good news. One, published just days before Anna left England for Canada, might have been a source of worry for Anna's mother. On May 28, 1917, the *Daily Gleaner* reported that two young soldiers had been killed in action. It also recorded that Sergeant Taylor of No. 8 Field Ambulance "has been notified that his sister, who was serving as nursing sister with the Canadian forces in France, has died as a result of illness following infection." No doubt, news of the illness and death of a nursing sister was difficult to read, and particularly worrisome for those families with daughters and sisters in service. If the story made Anna's family anxious for her safety, they did not have long to wait to hear first-hand about her experiences and make their own judgement about Anna's state of health.

On June 23, the Moncton *Daily Times* reported that Anna had "been successful in getting a leave of absence for seventeen days to spend at her home." It appears that Anna's family members might have alerted the newspaper of her arrival. The story further reported that "Miss Stamers will probably visit her aunt, Mrs. A.E. Killam, in Moncton, next week." On June 29, the newspaper duly recorded that Anna was a guest of her aunt for a few days. Although Anna was on leave after fifteen months of service at No. 1 CGH in Étaples, the paper erroneously stated that Anna had been transferred to No. 1 CCCS. The same day, on the next page, the comment that Anna had arrived in a Maritime port on a hospital ship was pure fiction.

Anna's time in Canada was clearly a welcome change, but she seems to have had little time to rest and forget, even for a moment, her wartime experiences. The following Friday, just a week after her arrival in New Brunswick, her Aunt Julia held a "Military at Home" in her honour. On Tuesday, July 3, the Moncton *Daily Times* reported every detail of her visit there: "On Friday afternoon Mrs. A.E. Killam received from 3 until 6 o'clock at her residence on Highfield Street in honour of her niece."

According to this account, the house was "prettily decorated with the flags of the allies," and, in addition to Anna's Aunt Julia, there were five others who "assisted in the tea room," two others who "ushered," and Mrs. Margaret Thompson "attended the door." The afternoon included musical entertainment from two soloists with their own accompanists as well as a reading. Although it did not report any of the details of Anna's talks or publish any photos, the newspaper reported that the ladies attending the "at home" showed great interest in Anna's souvenirs and photos. The next day, the paper reported that Anna and her family paid a visit to friends in Salisbury "one evening last week and made some social calls and received a warm welcome from their friends."

Anna's community was hungry for news, and presumably wanted to show their support for the work of their nursing sisters. The Saint John *Evening Times and Star* reported that Anna "fairly radiated British pluck and enthusiasm and was an inspiration to all with whom she came into contact." If that was the case, she must have put on a brave face. Perhaps even her family did not initially realize how tired she was. The next week, the *Daily Telegraph and The Sun* recorded that, on July 11, Anna spoke to the Red Cross Society in Chipman. According to the article, Anna "gave members of the society a slight idea of the work the Red Cross is doing at the front and a very clear statement of the things most needed for the work, which was very much appreciated by the members of the society here."

Anna was not the only nursing sister asked to speak to community groups. The New Brunswick dailies regularly reported on talks given by the nursing sisters. By 1917, support for the war was waning, and these talks might have become even more important. Certainly, members of the community who had family members in service would have been anxious for any first-hand accounts, however circumspect. The nursing sisters were not supposed to take photographs, although many did, nor were they supposed to be very specific in their descriptions. Nonetheless, the attendees no doubt found it reassuring to hear that the wounded were receiving good medical care and that their support was both needed and appreciated. Anna must have known that in 1915 and 1916 community members from Saint John had provided significant funding to build wooden huts at No. 1 CGH that offered better protection from the elements for the sick and wounded soldiers she nursed.

In between these social and speaking engagements Anna appeared before a Medical Board in Saint John the week before she was scheduled to leave. She might have recognized just how unwell she was, or someone else did. Officials at the hearing on July 3 found that she suffered from nervous exhaustion, irregular heartbeat, and sleeplessness, looked anemic, and assessed her general condition as poor. The Board attributed her health condition to overwork, and approved a period of rest commencing from that date until September 3. Anna must have been advised of their decision right away, since, after she spoke to the ladies in Chipman, the July 11 edition of the *Daily Telegraph and The Sun* reported that she had been granted a two-month leave of absence.

As it turned out, the Medical Board was slow in forwarding its findings to Ottawa—not sending the report until July 10, the day Anna's leave was due to expire. By then, the process for Anna and Jean to return to England was already set in motion. On the eleventh, a letter was sent to the Officer Commanding (OC) Discharge Depot in Quebec instructing that "Nursing Sister Jean Templeman report to Stewart Montreal Docks evening twentieth...and Nursing Sister A I Stamers embark same vessel at Quebec afternoon 21st." Anna must have received this direction by cable, since she sent a wire advising that she had been approved for two months' sick leave. The OC Discharge Depot, Quebec, advised Ottawa on the thirteenth that Anna had informed them of her approved leave, but still asked if she should sail as ordered or await further instruction. On July 18, the Adjutant General Canadian Military sent a letter enclosing the Medical Board's report to OC Halifax, and Ottawa subsequently informed London the same day. The problem was simply that correspondence between the Medical Board in Saint John, the Discharge Depot in Quebec, Ottawa, and London was not shared on a timely basis. When she was finally notified that she did not have to leave is not clear. At least for the next week, Anna was no doubt anxious that she had to return to England even though the Medical Board had judged her unwell. This problem of internal communication would resurface when Anna returned to England in September, and almost resulted in her being struck off strength or released from service.

Anna evidently spent the second half of July and the month of August resting and recovering her health. No further newspaper reports of her having speaking engagements were recorded. In late August, Anna appeared again before the Medical Board in Saint John, which found that, "at present, the general condition is good, tremors have disappeared, gained some weight." The Board determined that she had recovered and could resume duties. Part of its role was to recommend what type of service she was suited for: general service, service abroad, home service (Canada only), or temporarily unfit. The Board recommended that Anna be assigned to general service.

Just before she was scheduled to leave Saint John, two special events took place. On August 30, the *Daily Telegraph and The Sun* reported that Anna's home church, the Central Baptist Church, had held a farewell reception in her honour. "Her friends made this the occasion of both a welcome and a farewell." Mrs. R.D. Christie, President of the Willing Workers of Central Baptist Church, gave an address thanking Anna for her service during the prior two years. Mrs. D.J. MacPherson expressed appreciation for "the noble service rendered to the boys at the front by Miss Stamers," and included best wishes for her future work. Before the event concluded, "Little Esther Logue presented Anna with a bouquet of American beauty roses as a thank you to the brave young nurse." Reverend D.J. MacPherson offered a prayer, with music by Misses Gladys Goodner, Mildred Brown, and Roy Edwards, followed by refreshments. Anna expressed her thanks, "in a brief way outlined her work at the front," and passed around interesting snapshots of scenes "in war-ridden France." None of the photographs Anna shared was published in the story. She told those in attendance that she "expects to leave shortly on her return to duty at the front."

Finally, on September 1, Anna was a guest speaker at the meeting of the St. John Public Hospital Nurses Alumnae. Mrs. B. Howe hosted the meeting at her home on Elliott Row. The *Daily Telegraph and The Sun* reported that Anna "entertained the nurses by relating some of her experiences which proved one of the most enjoyable features of the evening." Together these events gave Anna the opportunity to speak to her church community and her professional colleagues about her work and the importance of their support for the war effort.

Anna's leave expired on September 3, but she did not leave Canada that day as planned. When their leaves were about to conclude, nursing sisters expected to be told when they were to sail and to receive train tickets to the port of departure. Anna's departure, however, was delayed by more administrative issues that nearly marred her record of service.

The process of arranging her return was not set in motion until after her leave expired. On September 7, the Director General Supplies Transport, Ottawa, sent a night letter to the OC Discharge Depot, Quebec, requiring Anna "to report to Leonard afternoon 20th instant." On September 15, the Assistant Director Medical Services asked the Secretary, Military Council, Ottawa, to arrange for Anna to return overseas. Precisely when Anna got the word is not clear, but sometime in mid-September she received the necessary directions as to where and when she was to proceed for embarkation. On September 18, the Moncton *Daily Times* reported that "Nursing Sister Stamers, who has been home on leave for two months, will arrive in Moncton from St. John this afternoon and will sail shortly from a Canadian port on her return overseas. She will leave Moncton this evening." Anna had the benefit of an additional two weeks in Canada as these administrative matters were concluded.

While Anna was en route to England, more confusion reigned over her leave between the officials responsible for her assignments. The Secretary Overseas Medical Forces in London, Captain MacKay, had not received notice that her original leave had been extended, despite his written inquiries. On October 2, MacKay wrote that Anna would be struck off strength effective September 3 "on being reported an absentee." By then, Anna was already en route to England and might have already arrived, although her arrival date is also not clear from her service file. The Matron, DMS Canadian Contingents, confirmed to MacKay that Anna had proceeded on transport duty to Canada on June 9, after which she was granted seventeen days' leave on arrival, and that her leave had been further extended to September 3 by the Medical Board. She also stated that Anna had been unable to obtain return transportation until September 20, and said that Anna "reported to us on October 10th."

In fact, Anna had not departed Montreal on September 20 nor likely shortly thereafter. According to the Incoming Passenger Lists for the United Kingdom and Ireland, Anna travelled to England aboard the RMS *Missanabie* of the Canadian Pacific Railway Steamship Line, and arrived at Liverpool on October 9. She was one of two nursing sisters among nineteen named passengers, mainly civilians. The manifest also notes a "Draft of fifty officers, Royal Flying Corps." The date of departure is not given, but it is likely that Anna returned to England in a transatlantic convoy, making the passage under anti-submarine escort at the speed of the slowest ship. With heightened U-boat activity in 1917, convoys had become the norm.

Again, as had been the case in 1915, Anna's directions did not specify where she was to go upon arrival. Nonetheless, the authorities needed to confirm that Anna had complied with her orders. On October 18, her matron wrote to Captain MacKay assuring him that the explanation provided by the two nurses, Anna and her colleague, F. Beauchesne, "for failure to report on the expiry of their leave were in every way satisfactory." Moreover, she reported that "transportation facilities have been so difficult recently that the delay in some officers returning from Canada have been unavoidable." That ended the matter for the military administrators and left Anna's record of service in good standing.

Anna's next set of instructions from the Militia and Defence Department were very clear. On October 12, she and a colleague, G. McCulloch, were advised that "you have been detailed to duty at No. 16 CGH Orpington." Further, "you should proceed by train leaving Cannon Street at 3:40 on the 12th." They were provided with a railway warrant for the journey "to be exchanged at the station for a ticket," and directed to report to Matron Smith.

Anna's family did not get news of her safe arrival for several days. On October 16, the Moncton *Daily Times* finally reported that "Mrs. B.A. Stamers, of St. John, who is the guest of her sister, Mrs. A.E. Killam, received a cable yesterday from London, of the safe arrival of daughter, Nursing Sister Stamers, who left about four weeks ago." By October 12, Anna was already at No. 16 CGH in Orpington, so it is not clear why she did not send a cable for several days.

When she arrived, Anna found that Jean Templeman had also been reassigned to No. 16 CGH, where she would spend the next six months. In 1915, the Ontario government had committed to set up and pay for a hospital to help meet the needs of the wounded and sick. It was formally opened as the Ontario Military Hospital in February 1916 by Colonial Secretary Andrew Bonar Law, the same month Anna left Moore Barracks for France, to serve Canadians and "other Colonials and Imperials." Unlike many military hospitals in England, which were converted sites, the Ontario Military Hospital was built from the ground up, although it was still a series of separate buildings as was the case at Moore Barracks. The hospital was staffed by mid-April 1916, and the first wounded and sick were admitted on June 8.

The work at No. 16 CGH must have been a welcome change from the trying conditions Anna experienced in the tent hospitals of France. When she arrived, the hospital was a modern, purpose-built, albeit temporary, facility. When it opened as the Ontario Military Hospital, eighty-one nursing sisters from Canada were on the Nominal Roll. By the fall of 1917, when Anna was reassigned there, the hospital had doubled in size and staff, and been renamed No. 16 Canadian General Hospital. Although the nursing sisters were mainly from Ontario, among them was New Brunswicker Isobel Draffin, of Rothesay.

During its first six months of operation in early 1916 the staff published a newsletter, the *Ontario Stretcher*, to describe its facilities for Canadians back home. Unlike the tent hospitals in France, the hospital consisted of small, wooden buildings. The wards were arranged in pairs, and the space between the wards covered, so that it was possible to move between wards and stay dry. Each ward contained fifty beds and had its own kitchen, pantry, medicine room, nursing sisters' chart room, bath, and washroom. The hospital also included a Recreation Room that also served as a church, theatre, concert hall, and lounge with a seating

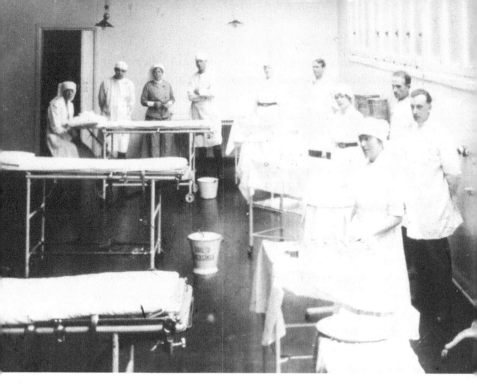

Operating Room, Ontario Military Hospital.

capacity of four hundred, a Patient's Canteen, and a Billiard and Reading Room. Close to the Recreation Room was an admitting room with ten large bathtubs and an abundance of hot water, soap, and towels. Four other buildings contained the Operating Theatre, X-ray Room, Anesthetic and Sterilizing Rooms, and Wash and Dressing Rooms. The administration building was close by, as were the quarters for the officers and nursing sisters, "all large, comfortable and well adapted to meet the needs of the large hospital staff." The hospital also had its own butcher shop, bakery, and a dining room with a seating capacity of four hundred. Most significantly, the hospital was steam-heated, lit by electricity, and directly connected to the London County Council's sewage, water, and gas supply system. Further, the hospital's location meant that the wounded could be transported by train from Folkestone to No. 16 CGH in about an hour.

By all accounts the work environment was collegial, and the staff was proud of the facility and anxious to let Canadians know how their tax funds were being used. Nurses were among the contributors to the *Ontario Stretcher*. One was Nursing Sister Marion Gertrude Stovel, of Stratford, Ontario, who was given prominence in the first issue. Each subsequent issue included a column entitled "as the nursing sisters see it." Although they did not necessarily have an equal voice, their views were being sought and validated by having the column.

When Anna arrived at No. 16 CGH in October, several nursing sisters she had served with at Moore Barracks and No. 1 CGH had also been transferred there. Although she was no longer with her friends Ethel and Nellie, she no doubt made new friends. She was also busy. The demand for care was so great that, within a few weeks, they had 2,080 patients. As her experience at No. 1 CGH demonstrated, there were times when patients were quickly evacuated to England from base hospitals in France to free up space there. In this case, the pressure came during the Third Battle of Ypres, which had begun in late July with British attacks. The Canadians went into the line in October, eventually capturing the shattered village of Passchendaele that lent its name to the battle. Given the push to move patients from general hospitals in France to those in England, the well-equipped and well-staffed No. 16 CGH must have relieved some of the pressure on the facilities on the Western Front.

To cope with the increased demand, the nursing establishment increased to 127, including Anna. She encountered soldiers from throughout the British Empire. During 1917, 9,912 patients were admitted, almost half of whom were Canadians (4,571), followed by "Imperials" (British, 4,587), Australians (752), and two soldiers from New Zealand. During 1918, a further 10,452 patients were admitted with similar percentages of countries of origin. Intense fighting on the Western Front began again in late March and went on, largely unabated, until the armistice in November 1918. Anna's time at No. 16 included both of these busy periods in 1917 and 1918.

Although Anna was now away from the front and no longer had to confront the terrible state of incoming wounded, No. 16 had its own challenges. Like Moore Barracks, it was set up to receive patients who had already undergone medical treatment in France. Nonetheless, it was a full-service hospital. The war diary for No. 16 CGH shows that, in 1917, 1,338 major operations were performed and in 1918 a further 1,339. Dr. Bruce Robertson, an Ontario physician who pioneered blood transfusions for wounded soldiers, served at No. 16 CGH, while R. Thomas McRae, brother of Dr. John McRae who wrote "In Flanders Fields," was a plastic surgeon there. Many of the 4,320 surgeries performed between April 1916 and the end of the war were done to restore some normality to soldiers with severe disfigurements. These patients, and the nursing sisters who cared for them, had to confront the fact that these men had life-limiting or life-altering wounds. Such patients might well have remained at No. 16 CGH for longer than at hospitals at the front, affording the

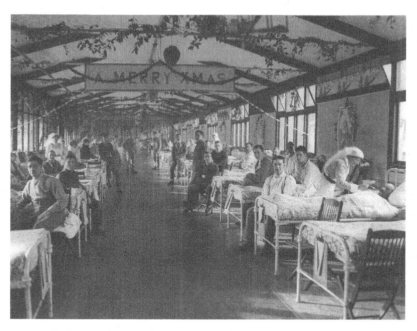

Patients, visitors, and nurses, No. 16 Canadian Military Hospital, Christmas 1918. Canadian Expeditionary Force photograph albums, C 224-8, Archives of Ontario, I0004870

nurses more opportunity to provide ongoing care. Once these serious cases were stabilized, it was common to send them home for further treatment and convalescence. No. 16 CGH sent 4,929 invalids to Canada.

No. 16 CGH differed significantly from Anna's previous assignments in many other ways. It was much closer to London and situated in a beautiful part of England, farther away from the risk of air raids. Anna spent Christmas 1917 there, and in January 1918 her thirtieth birthday. Anna's service file does not show any significant leave while at No. 16, although technically she would have been eligible again only in January 1918 because of her extended leave the previous summer. According to Clare Gass, if the workload permitted, the nurses were granted a half-day leave every two weeks. Since Orpington was accessible by train and a short distance from London, Anna might well have taken advantage of its proximity to visit. If she did, no letters or record of any such visits have been identified.

During 1917, Anna's decision to serve as a nursing sister gave her an unexpected opportunity beyond caring for the sick and wounded: for the first time in her life, she would have the right to vote in a federal election. In fact, there was much political discussion among the nursing sisters of No. 16 CGH that year. In August, a nursing sister from Alberta, Roberta MacAdams, ran for office in her home province and won. Anna did not arrive until after MacAdams's victory, but surely her election in the summer must have animated the political discussion in the nursing sisters' mess as the federal election approached in the latter part of 1917.

By fall 1917, when the *Military Voters Act* became law, Canada had been at war for three years. Passed by Prime Minister Robert Borden's Union government, the act was an attempt to gain support for his government, which was struggling after introducing conscription in May. The act gave the right to vote to all Canadians serving overseas, and nursing sisters got the vote by virtue of their status as officers in the military. The legislation also gave the vote to female relatives of Canadian soldiers serving overseas — in Anna's case, this right was extended to her mother, Lavinia, and her two sisters, Gladys and Willa. The government issued a poster, "Enfranchised Women!" that confirmed who could vote and what

"Enfranchised Women!"
voting poster.

ENFRANCHISED WOMEN!

Women of Canada enfranchised for the purposes of the pending federal election are:

First—Nurses serving overseas with the Canadian or the Imperial forces.

Second—Next-of-kin of soldiers and nurses, living or dead, who are serving or have served during the present war overseas with the Canadian or the Imperial forces, and of sailors, living or dead, who have served or are serving during the present war with the fleet, either in Canadian or other waters.

The kinship must be of blood, and of the degree of wife, mother, sister or daughter. Half-sisters are regarded as full sisters under the Act and are entitled to the same franchise privileges.

All the relatives of the degrees enunciated may claim the franchise, and none others.

Women to vote must be of the full age of 21 years. British subjects by birth or naturalization and must be resident in Canada one year and in the electoral division three months. They must have their names on the voters' list. This list will be posted in each electoral division December 2.

Next-of-kin, see that your names are listed.

But to VOTE you must REGISTER.

It is your immediate duty, and very simple. Go to your nearest registration office and have your name put on the list. The local Unionist Committee will tell you where. DO IT NOW.

REGISTER FIRST—THEN VOTE—FOR THE BOYS AT THE FRONT.

VOTE UNION
SAVE CANADA

the requirements were. Should there be any doubt, the poster stated in bold lettering, "VOTE UNION. SAVE CANADA."

The government's decision to give these women the right to vote was more pragmatic than progressive. It was critical for the Borden government to be able to recruit more soldiers, as, by late 1916, the enthusiasm with which men had volunteered for service had waned in the face of the reality of the war. As Katherine Dewar notes, "[t]he passion for King and country was inversely proportional to the number of maimed and mangled bodies returning home and the increased public awareness of the war's high casualty counts." In the eleven months ending in November 1917, only 22,487 men enlisted in the CEF; in the same period, there were 119,541 casualties. Borden felt that the only way to keep Canada in the

Nursing Sister Alma Finnie (left) casting the first female vote at
No. 16 CGH, December 1917. LAC-M-381C, Library and Archives Canada

fight was to adopt conscription for overseas service. The men and women
of the CEF agreed with him: the overseas military election results were
215,000 votes for conscription and 20,000 against. The *Canadian Nurse*
reported that more than 500,000 women voted on December 17, 1917,
and Borden further promised women universal suffrage, "a promise he
kept in 1918."

Much fanfare accompanied this historic moment, including government photographers who recorded it at polling booths set up at CAMC
hospitals. Three Ontario nursing sisters who were Anna's colleagues at
No. 16 CGH were photographed while casting their ballots: Alma Finnie,
Oda Weldon, and Jean Bennett, the first nursing sisters to vote. According
to Pat Staton, the Canadian suffragette Nellie McClung had a son in
the trenches and urged women to use their vote to support conscription.

Staton argues that the suffragists and government both recognized the power that their war work gave women.

Clare Gass, who had moved to No. 2 CCS in France, was preoccupied with the risk of bombs during this period, not the prospect of voting. On December 3, she noted: "Fritz has been overhead all night tonight....I have got several cases in from the bombs which were dropped. They fell in a camp near Pop [Poperinghe]. Where the Midland Regt are billeted." On the fifth, she recorded: "Today about noon the Germans began to shell the Crossroads again...another shell burst just outside No. 3's mess hut....I was asleep when the shelling began but the whir of the first shell overhead awakened me. The explosions shook the ground." Like the majority of those close to the front, Clare voted for conscription. "I voted for the Union Government in Canada — this a.m." Ella Mae Bongard, a Canadian serving with the US Army, was more enthusiastic about the opportunity. She wrote: "Dec. 9/17 Voted tonight in the Canadian elections. A Canadian officer came out from Havre to arrange it. I feel quite important now. You may be sure I voted for conscription despite party politics for I don't want to see Canada drop out of the war at this stage." It seems that Ella saw the significance of her vote in the immediate context of the war and as support for the war effort. If she saw it as a step toward rights for women generally, she did not express it.

We do not know for sure, but it is likely that Anna and her friends exercised their franchise. They had already given nearly three years of their lives to the war effort and suffered considerable hardship. Moreover, they had cared for many young soldiers and seen the toll the fighting had taken on them. Like Ella, they will have wanted to see fresh recruits to ensure a final, favourable resolution to this devastating war. Anna's mother, Lavinia, and her sisters, Gladys and Willa, also likely exercised their right to vote — no doubt they will have wished to see the war end as much as any family with loved ones overseas.

Compared to No. 1 CGH in Étaples, No. 16 CGH was a much more pleasant atmosphere, away from the pressures of the front and with comfortable living and working conditions. Nevertheless, Anna and her colleagues had lived through a very trying period since leaving Canada.

Clare Gass's diary entry to begin 1918 reflects on what she—and Anna— had experienced since mid-1915. The entry alludes to scripture, showing both Clare's despair and her resolve. The passage begins: "The Cup of War. Are ye able to drink of the cup that I shall drink of? And they said unto him, We are able." The text, from Matthew 20:22, would have been familiar to Anna, and she would have understood Clare's meaning. The scripture refers to "The Cup of Suffering," but Clare changed it to "The Cup of War." In the passage she quotes, Jesus has just predicted his own

Matron H. Smith (left), ca. 1916-19.

suffering and coming crucifixion. When a woman approaches him and seeks reassurance that her sons will have eternal life, Jesus replies, "Ye know not what ye ask. Are ye able to drink of the cup that I shall drink of?" And they said unto him "We are able." By this point in the war, Clare had lost a brother and cousin in the Battle of Vimy Ridge and another brother, Cyril, had his foot amputated. She had endured much since she had been taken on strength, yet, in using this passage, Clare seems to be saying that, despite the suffering, she will go on. In 1914, when Colonel Jones spoke to the recruits, he had said that military nursing required three attributes: "Coolness, Courage and Skill." He might well have included a fourth: Resilience.

Like Clare, Anna had a religious background, and this no doubt sustained her through many of the experiences. Friendships also gave her strength. In the time she served at No. 16 CGH, she was in the company of her good friend and colleague Jean Templeman and many other women she had worked with at Moore Barracks and No. 1 CGH in France. Among the latter when Anna arrived were Mary Domville and Edith McCafferty. Isobel Draffin and Dr. Margaret Parks also spent time at No. 16 CGH when she first arrived. During her time there, Anna served under Matron H. Smith, who completed a performance appraisal for Anna's file. As in her previous one at Moore Barracks, there is not a lot of narrative. There is no indication of whether Anna had the opportunity to discuss her performance appraisal, and she did not sign it. It confirms that Anna commenced her duties on October 12 and Matron Smith was her supervisor throughout her service there. Anna was assessed in seven areas, including nursing capability, administrative capability, and tact-personality. In the category of special qualifications and suitability for emergency work, Matron Smith wrote, "unable to state." While her nursing capabilities were "good," Smith noted that Anna "did not keep a very tidy ward." Presumably, this was the reason she gave her a "fairly good" rating on administrative capability. Where it mattered most, however, on the care of her patients, Anna's rating was "very good," and her personality was described as "gentle and kind." This performance appraisal and the one from Moore Barracks are the most objective assessments on record of the type of person Anna was and how she performed as a nursing sister.

In 1917 and 1918, there was a significant influx of nursing sisters into the CAMC — according to Cynthia Toman, 596 in 1917 and a further 499 in 1918 — helping to relieve Anna and her colleagues to be posted to less demanding assignments. By the spring of 1918, Anna had worked at two general hospitals in England, served on the Western Front for fifteen months, and been part of the war effort for almost three years. There was a logical connection between No. 16 CGH and the hospital ships that transported severely wounded or incapacitated soldiers home for convalescence: No. 16 CGH sent nearly five thousand soldiers back to Canada between June 1916 and September 1919. On March 22, 1918, the day after the great German Spring Offensive was unleashed on the Western Front, Anna, Jean Templeman, Carola Douglas, Minnie Follette, and Mae Belle Sampson were all assigned to His Majesty's Hospital Ship *Llandovery Castle*. Anna would again be among friends.

Chapter Seven

Life and Death on a Hospital Ship:
The Risks and the Rules

By the time Anna was transferred to *Llandovery Castle* in late March 1918, wounded and sick Canadian soldiers had been travelling home on board hospital ships for much of the war. That month, Canada took over responsibility for staffing the British *Llandovery Castle* and the repatriation of Canadian convalescent soldiers. This would be Anna's last and, as it turned out, most dangerous assignment with the CAMC. It also brought her to the attention of the world.

The role of the hospital ship was to transport wounded and sick soldiers for treatment or back home to recover or be discharged. No one expected hospital ships to be at risk. Winston Churchill, First Lord of the Admiralty from 1912 until 1915, reflected the common belief that Germany "would have to flout International Law and the accepted customs of the sea (as expressed in the Geneva Convention/Hague Conferences of 1899 and 1907)" if it were to use submarines against non-naval targets. Submarines were entitled to stop non-naval ships and capture them, but only after boarding and searching them to establish the identity and nature of the cargo. Ships could not simply be sunk on sight, nor could they be sunk without provision for the safety of the crew and passengers.

International law made attacks on Allied merchant shipping problematic for Germany. Twice, in 1915 and again in 1916, it had tried to

VICTORY
BONDS
WILL HELP STOP
· THIS ·

KULTUR VS. HUMANITY.

establish a blockade around Britain by sinking ships without warning. In both cases, the reaction of the United States forced Germany to abandon the attempt. The declaration of an unrestricted submarine campaign in February 1917 was undertaken in the full knowledge that the United States would declare war. Germany's hope was that it could win before American troops arrived in force on the Western Front.

By 1917, the risk posed by German U-boats was a very real concern, even to hospital ships. According to Jonathan Johnson, the first hospital ship to cross the Atlantic to Canada was HMHS *Essequibo* in 1917. Nursing Sister Winnifred Dobson Schurman, from Prince Edward Island, was on board *Essequibo* when the German U-54 intercepted it. Katherine Dewar recounts Schurman's experience. They were "somewhere off the coast of Ireland" when someone spotted a German submarine sailing toward them. The nursing sisters donned their lifebelts and waited as the submarine came alongside and a German party boarded. After an hour and a half of interrogation, the Germans returned to their submarine, hoisted a flag "signalling bon voyage" and the captain of *Essequibo* did the same. Schurman described the tension among the nursing sisters: "the nerve strain of that hour and a half was awful...no one fainted...there was no hysteria or anything of the sort...everyone was as quiet and calm as could be." When they reached their port of call that evening, they attended a church service "to rejoice in their good fortune and to thank God for their lives." In fact, the interaction between *Essequibo* and U-54 as described by Schurman is exactly as it should have unfolded under international law.

Hospital ships had been given special protection under the 1907 Hague Convention, to which Germany, Britain, and all the naval powers were signatories. Articles 1-3 required that before their use as hospital ships, the names of ships constructed or fitted for such service were to be communicated to the belligerent powers. If the ship was provided by

(opposite): Propaganda poster depicting the German U-boat
attack on HMHS *Llandovery Castle*.

private individuals or relief societies, it had to be under the control of a belligerent power. Article 4 required that registered hospital ships assist the sick, wounded, and shipwrecked of all belligerents irrespective of nationality. The hospital ship could not be used for any military purpose nor could it hamper the movements of combatants. The article also gave belligerents the right to control and search the ship, make it take a certain course, and in certain circumstances detain it. Author Stephen McGreal notes that, although Article 4 mandated that hospital ships were subject to visits and inspections, submarine commanders seldom exercised this right because it risked signalling their presence. Article 5 required that military hospital ships be painted white with a horizontal green stripe and fly "the white flag with a red cross" to identify them as protected vessels. Under no circumstances could a "sink first, ask questions later" approach be justified. As McGreal succinctly explains it, "[t]he Geneva Convention is essentially a recommended listing of dos and do nots to ensure a fair play between foes in times of war, but a great deal depended on how an enemy interpreted a particular section of the code of conduct."

Article 1 of the Convention stipulating that hospital ships were not to be used for any other purpose was put to the test early in the war. On October 17, 1914, the British cruiser *Undaunted* attacked and destroyed a half-flotilla of German minelayers. Although the British rescued many survivors, the Germans sent in their hospital ship, the *Ophelia*, to pick up others. According to Macphail, the *Ophelia* was fitted up as a hospital ship and bore all the requisite markings, but the British captured it, claiming that it had been sent in for scouting purposes. The case went before the Prize Court, which concluded that the *Ophelia* was being used as a signalling ship and had never attempted to act as a hospital ship. Still, the Germans contended it was a hospital ship, and German Admiral Reinhard Scheer later argued that, after this, "we also considered ourselves released from our obligations and with far more justification took action against hospital ships, which under cover of the Red Cross flag, were patently used for the transport of troops." According to Macphail, the Germans used the case of the *Ophelia* to justify their actions against British hospital ships in almost every instance thereafter.

Hospital ships were soon caught up in the conflict over access to maritime waters in and around Britain and the Mediterranean. In October 1914, the British had imposed a naval blockade against Germany and her allies, which exceeded the international limit on contraband items (materials used expressly for military purposes) and extended it to imports of food, chemicals, fertilizer, and other items used by civilians—as well as war industry and the military. The Germans responded by attempting to establish their own blockade of Britain using submarines. On February 4, 1915, notice was given in the *Imperial Gazette* that "the waters around Great Britain and Ireland are declared in the war zone." All ships inside the war zone were now vulnerable to attack. On the same day, instructions were given to German commanders that "hospital ships are to be spared; they may only be attacked when they are obviously used for the transport of troops from England to France."

In the early years of the war this commitment was honoured. In 1915, Hubert Chitty, a surgeon working on a hospital ship, published an article in the *British Medical Journal* claiming that hospital ships were not at risk: "Fortunately, our work has been carried out in security. It has never been hampered by any disregard, on the part of the enemy, of the Geneva Convention. The Turks are, from all accounts, remarkably clean fighters. They certainly respect hospitals and hospital ships." There had, however, already been an attack. On February 1, 1915, a German torpedo narrowly missed the British hospital ship *Asturias*. The next day, the French Ministry of Marine declared that the action was a violation of the Hague Convention, and the British Admiralty gave the press details based on statements by the master and two officers, who confirmed that they had sighted the track of the torpedo, the wash of the periscope in their wake, and the submarine as it followed them. Chastened, the German Embassy in Washington issued an apology, contending that the U-boat had mistaken it for a transport ship, even though it bore Red Cross markings and hospital ship lighting.

In 1916, however, the Germans began sinking hospital ships. On March 17, the Russian hospital ship *Portugal* was torpedoed by U-33 in the Black Sea. Fortunately, *Portugal* was not carrying wounded at the

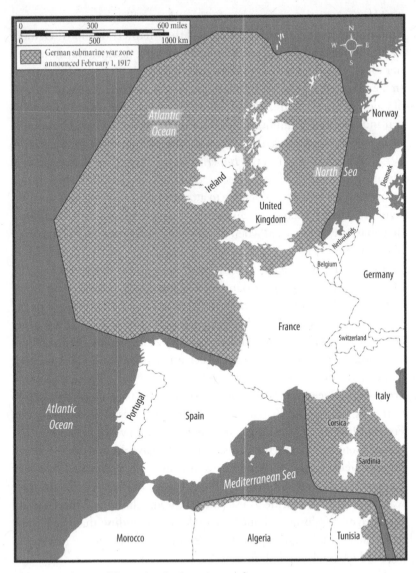

Unrestricted submarine warfare. Mike Bechthold

time, but eighty-five lives were lost: forty-five of the victims were Red Cross staff, fifteen of them women. Then, when the Germans torpedoed *Portugal*'s replacement, the hospital ship *Vpered*, seven more men lost their lives. These ships were targeted even though they bore all the distinguishing marks of a hospital ship as required under the Convention.

By 1917, Germany had endured two and a half years of Britain's economic blockade and had failed to negotiate a peace settlement. The Germans did not have enough resources to feed their people and continue the war. On January 31, 1917, they announced their decision to engage in unrestricted submarine warfare, effective the next day. This meant that German submarines would attempt to sink every ship in a declared war zone around Britain and France and in the Mediterranean. In 1915, they had made an exception for hospital ships, but with the 1917 policy there would be no exceptions. The Germans contended that they had conclusive proof of the misuse of hospital ships for the transport of munitions and troops. Consequently, the Germans stated emphatically that the traffic of hospital ships "would no longer be tolerated." This declaration of intent also meant they could no longer argue that any attacks were mistakes. Article 4 of the Convention gave them the authority to search any ship for proof, present this proof, and seek a legal remedy. They would no longer follow this course. In fact, the practice of arming British merchant ships and their willingness to fight back when a U-boat was sighted made it dangerous for German submariners to follow the Hague Convention. The German solution to this dilemma in 1917 was to shoot on sight.

The British response was to deny flatly that they misused hospital ships and to argue that, if the Germans believed this, they had recourse under international law. In addition to their denials, the British used other tactics to refute the allegations, essentially starting a public relations campaign. In 1917, they published a white paper in which they addressed all the allegations of the German government. The report refuted claims made in four categories: alleged excessive use of hospital ships in the Gallipoli campaign, changes in the listing of hospital ships with the intention to deceive, transport of munitions, and transport of troops. The

Foreign Office forwarded a copy of the white paper to the British Embassy in Washington on November 21. Once again, as McGreal relates, the British pointed out that "German warships never once exercised their right of inspection to verify their suspicion. Instead of giving His Majesty's government an opportunity to rebut these allegations, they proceeded to ruthlessly attack innocent hospital ships engaged in the humane task of carrying the sick and the wounded."

Another text, "The War on Hospital Ships," published in Britain in 1917, sets out the case that hospital ships were deliberately being targeted by the Germans. Described as a narrative of eyewitnesses, it recounts the details of ships targeted beginning with *Portugal* in March 1916 to HMHS *Gloucester Castle* in March 1917. It includes the statement of the International Committee of the Red Cross following the German declaration of unrestricted submarine warfare. The report also points out that wounded Germans taken prisoner were being transported on hospital ships, and that actions against these ships were actions against their own men. It would appear to have been written to draw the attention of the international community to the ongoing threat to the lives of non-combatants. Clearly, it was important for the British to refute the allegations that they were misusing hospital ships in violation of international law. If they could not get before a tribunal to argue against German tactics, they would use the court of public opinion.

In early 1917, the International Red Cross denounced the actions of the German government following the torpedoing of the hospital ships *Asturias*, *Britannic*, and *Gloucester Castle*. Citing its duty to enforce the principles of the Red Cross and international law, the Red Cross, based in Geneva, stated that Germany's resolution "is in contradiction to the humanitarian conventions which it has pledged itself to solemnly respect." The communique went on to charge: "In torpedoing hospital ships it is not attacking combatants, but defenseless beings wounded or mutilated in war, and women who are devoting themselves to the work of relief and charity."

In 1917, the Americans reached the same conclusion. For two years, the United States had maintained a neutral position in the struggle between Britain and the Triple Alliance. In 1915, the Germans deliberately torpedoed the *Lusitania*, a British passenger ship with many Americans on board, yet the Americans did not change their position of neutrality. They were appeased when the German high command ordered their U-boat commanders to cease targeting merchant ships in September 1915. The Americans retreated again in spring 1916, when the Germans sank a number of cross-channel passenger steamers. When the Germans torpedoed and sank the French-flagged passenger ferry *Sussex,* as many as one hundred crew and passengers lost their lives. Although there were Americans on board, they were not among the lost.

Then, the German announcement on January 31, 1917, to pursue unrestricted warfare brought condemnation from the United States, which severed diplomatic relations with Germany. By early April, the Americans had finally made their decision to declare war. On April 2, in his "War Message" to Congress, President Woodrow Wilson cited the extraordinary nature of Germany's decision "to put aside all restraints of law or of humanity and use its submarines to sink every vessel." According to Wilson, this policy shift swept every restriction aside when even hospital ships and ships carrying relief to the sorely bereaved and stricken people of Belgium would be subject to destruction. The German policy meant a "wanton and wholesale destruction of the lives of non-combatants, men, women and children, engaged in pursuits which have always, even in the darkest periods of modern history, been deemed innocent and legitimate.... The present German submarine warfare against commerce is warfare against mankind."

Part of Wilson's rationale for war was the egregious action taken by the Germans against hospital ships, an argument that resonated with this humanitarian and principled president. They torpedoed two hospital ships just days before Wilson gave his address, and two others followed within two weeks: HMHS *Asturias* was torpedoed by UC-66 on March 20, and HMHS *Gloucester Castle* by UC-56 on March 30. Shortly afterwards, HMHS *Lanfranc* was sunk by UB-40 and HMHS *Donegal* by UC-21, both on April 17. In all cases, lives were lost. This pattern continued in 1918 with the destruction of as many as six more hospital ships.

The British continued to invoke the protections of the Hague Convention for hospital ships, despite growing evidence in 1917 that the Germans did not feel bound by it. The British had little recourse. Patients had to be evacuated by hospital ship from the "killing fields of France and Belgium" and elsewhere to be cared for, initially on the Continent, and then transported to England or elsewhere for recovery. This was the state of affairs on March 22, when Anna was assigned to HMHS *Llandovery Castle*.

Llandovery Castle was launched in 1913 as a mail steamer for the Union Castle Line. At a little over 10,000 tons displacement and a speed of fifteen knots, it carried passengers and mail between London and Africa before being acquired by the British government and recommissioned as a hospital ship on July 26, 1916. The Union Castle Line supplied nineteen ships during the war, thirteen of which were used as hospital ships. According to McGreal, before the war was over, Union Castle hospital ships brought 354,000 British wounded and over 9,000 enemy wounded to Southampton. Ships sometimes alternated roles between mail ship, troopship, and hospital ship. When serving as hospital ships, however, they had to be painted with the requisite markings, fly the flag of the International Red Cross, and be registered as a hospital ship, and the opposing party had to be so notified.

After being converted to a hospital ship, *Llandovery Castle* had capacity for 658 patients and accommodation for medical staff and crew. The ship made two trips to Canada staffed with British medical personnel, the first in September 1917 and the second in February 1918. The first trip brought 629 sick and wounded home and the second carried another 648 soldiers to Canadian soil. In 1918, the Canadian government chartered *Llandovery Castle* to convey sick and wounded military personnel from England to Halifax. Over the course of its career as a hospital ship, *Llandovery Castle* carried 3,223 patients in five voyages.

No doubt her appointment to *Llandovery Castle* was exciting news for Anna and her family, since it allowed her to travel regularly to Canada. Yet, by 1918, they also would have known that hospital ships had been torpedoed and sunk. Sometime in March, Anna wrote to tell her mother about her new assignment. Perhaps to reassure her mother that she was among friends, she named her colleagues. Hospital ships typically were staffed with fourteen nursing sisters, but it appears that the team was not finalized when Anna wrote home. She listed her nursing sister colleagues as Miss Doucette (Alexina Dussault), Montreal; Miss McLean, Prince Edward Island; Miss Sampson, Miss Gallagher [sic, Gallaher], Ottawa; Miss Campbell, Miss McKenzie, Miss Follette, Springhill, Nova Scotia; and Miss Templeman. Carola Douglas joined in March, although Anna never mentioned her in her letter to her mother. Nursing Sister Margaret Marjorie "Pearl" Fraser of New Glasgow, Nova Scotia, was acting matron.

In addition to Jean Templeman, Anna had worked with Minnie Follette of Wards Brook, Nova Scotia, at No. 16 CGH, Orpington. Minnie had experience on a hospital ship, having been aboard HMHS *Letitia* when it ran aground in Halifax. So, Anna was among friends, and those whom she mentioned in her letter to her mother remained with her on all three trips. Four of the nursing sisters had been in service since the war began; the others had joined in 1915. Clearly, they had all done their part for the war effort, and might have welcomed the opportunity to be away from the pressures of incoming wounded, despite the risks.

Anna also listed five CAMC medical officers on board: Captains Hutton, Shellington, and Leonard, as well as Majors Lyon and MacDonald. When *Llandovery Castle* was assigned to the Canadian government, Major Thomas MacDonald of Port Hawkesbury, Nova Scotia, was appointed officer-in-charge. Like the nursing sisters, there would be changes among the medical officers, and of those she listed, only now MacDonald (by then lieutenant-colonel) and Major Thomas Lyon remained by the third trip.

Not many nursing sisters served on a hospital ship and few such personal accounts survive. Anna served for only three months, and if she described any of her impressions of her work on board, her insights were never published. Maureen Duffus relates the experience of a Canadian nurse, Elsie Collis, who served on *Asturias* in March 1917. According to Elsie, "they had to sleep in [their] clothes as much as possible in case of accidents." On May 5, she recorded in her diary that a troopship with three thousand sailors and sixty nursing sisters aboard was torpedoed. She later confided her relief that, although the women lost everything, they were safe, and "everyone says the girls were splendid. Some rowed all the time until they were picked up." Despite the risks, it seems that the nursing sisters were resolute, and confident in the knowledge that should such a situation occur, they would have the courage to face it.

Cynthia Toman recounts the experience of Marion Ruddick on board HMHS *Araguaya* in September 1917. Ruddick's trip was a demanding one, as she had responsibility for seventy-nine severe surgical cases, including patients with paraplegia, fracture cases, and a pyloric cancer patient who had to be fed through an enterostomy (direct feeding through an opening into the small intestine). Ruddick's workload was made all the greater since the second nurse on her ward was off sick during the journey.

Another Canadian nursing sister wrote an article, published in June 1918, describing life on a hospital ship. Regarding risk, she offered some advice: "Before actually joining a ship, a Sister may feel apprehensive of the possibilities of encountering mines and submarines, but, once on board, it is curious how one never thinks of possible dangers. If they sometimes do cross one's mind, it is usually in conjunction with the fervent hope that, if a catastrophe should occur, the Sisters will not fail to act according to their past high traditions in this and former wars." Although the author minimized the risks of mines and submarines, she was less sanguine about other challenges, including seasickness: "Nursing on hospital ships tries the endurance of the best of sailors." She warned that sickness was often inevitable when working at high pressure "in stuffy airless wards with the portholes closed on account of heavy seas.... Seasickness is quite the biggest bugbear a Sister can face." She further noted that getting sick "is grossly unfair to our sick and wounded" when a sister might have to leave them at critical times.

Living conditions on the hospital ship were not necessarily worse or better than on land. The nursing sister just quoted also cautioned against "taking some cherished dress or coat," since it might get "eaten by the rats and cockroaches." In some instances, nurses were provided with separate cabins that could be "a place of refuge, however tiny" and a place to escape from "the ceaseless chattering of a tactless cabin-fellow." The nursing sister also described the challenges in teaching orderlies to make poultices, fomentation, and perform blanket baths: "It is sometimes difficult to make them realize that asepsis and antisepsis, and such like are of real importance and not merely a fad of doctors and sisters."

On March 28, 1918, Anna was on board when *Llandovery Castle* made its first trip as a Canadian hospital ship staffed by members of the CAMC. The ship left Liverpool and arrived in Halifax eleven days later, on April 7. How long they remained in port is not clear. The Moncton *Daily Times* reported on April 13, however, that Anna's mother, Lavinia, was now a guest of her sister, Mrs. E.A. Killam, having "returned from Halifax where she visited her daughter Anna, who is serving on a hospital ship." If Lavinia was in Halifax awaiting the arrival of the ship on the seventh and returned by train to Moncton on the twelfth, the ship was likely in port no more than four days. Still, this was the first chance for Anna and her mother to spend time together since Anna had returned to England in late September 1917.

Lavinia was nervous about Anna's new assignment. As the *Moncton Transcript* later reported, she met Anna on the ship, "a big white vessel, all shimmering in the night with electric lights and contrasting Red Cross emblems." Lavinia expressed her fears to Anna "that some day the boat with all its glare and emblazonments would easily attract the ruthless submarines and be sunk." Anna tried to reassure her mother: "Why mother dear…that's just why our ship is so brightly lighted and painted in white to show the enemy that we are hospital people and have a right for humanity's sake to go unmolested." Lavinia was not easily reassured, so Anna drew on their mutual spiritual beliefs saying, "Why, I am as safe on that ship as on land in my war work, and anyhow what does it matter, the same Great Hand governs both land and sea. I have my duty to perform. It will be all right in any case, Mother."

Nursing Sister Pauline Balloch, from Centreville, New Brunswick, also had to reassure her parents that she would arrive safely when she travelled to Canada on a hospital ship. It was common practice that, when nursing sisters were granted leave in Canada, they travelled on troopships or made their way "on command" on a hospital ship as their means of passage. Historian Ross Hebb confirms that Pauline was on board when *Llandovery Castle* made its first trip to Halifax in late March. She had been taken on strength at No. 16 CGH, Orpington, in June 1917 before being transferred to No. 1 CGH and other service in France. She had been granted fourteen days' leave in Canada to be with her ailing mother. She did not return on *Llandovery Castle*. Three other nursing sisters were assigned to *Llandovery Castle* on that first trip, but their identities are not certain.

When *Llandovery Castle* returned to England, there were additions to the nursing staff, but none of the original ten nurses was changed. Sophie Hoerner, the nursing sister from No. 3 CGH, also made the second trip "on command," a working passage on her way home for leave. She had served at No. 3 CCS from November 9, 1917, until April 21, 1918, when she was posted to the CAMC Depot. Sophie's leave in Canada commenced on May 16, the day after *Llandovery Castle* arrived. Sophie was not part of the nursing staff afterwards, and so was not on board for the fateful return trip in June.

Waiting for *Llandovery Castle* on this second arrival in Halifax was the ship's matron, Margaret Fraser. Tragedy had interrupted her service. On March 4, 1918, just before her appointment as acting matron of *Llandovery Castle*, her younger brother was killed in an enemy artillery barrage. Three weeks later, Matron Fraser was granted a month's sick leave. She probably made the first voyage to Canada on March 28, and took her leave when the ship arrived in Halifax on April 7. According to the ship's manifest, *Llandovery Castle* sailed from Halifax again on May 25, and it is likely that Acting Matron Fraser was aboard, as the timing of departure coincided with the end of her leave in mid-May.

After the ship returned to England, Anna's long-time friend and colleague Nellie Floyd joined her on *Llandovery Castle*. Nellie had remained at No. 1 CGH Étaples for a couple of months after Anna left, but they had not worked together since May 1917. While Anna was on leave in Canada in the summer of 1917, Nellie was assigned to a hospital in England and briefly assigned to the hospital ship HMHS *Araguaya*. In October, she was given leave and permission to travel to Canada. Like Anna, her leave was extended another month, and when she returned on January 8, 1918, she was posted to the Granville Special Hospital in Buxton, England. She remained there until May 2, when she was posted to *Llandovery Castle* as a masseuse, an early type of physiotherapy. Nellie and Anna, who had made their first voyage together on the RMS *Megantic* in 1915, were together again at sea.

When they arrived in Halifax in May, Anna and Nellie both travelled to New Brunswick. On May 17, the Moncton *Daily Times* reported that Anna and her friend "arrived in the city last night from an Atlantic port where the hospital ship on which she is engaged, recently docked." The paper further reported: "they leave today for St. John and leave again at once to re-join the hospital ship." The Saint John *Evening Times and Star* later recorded: "Nursing Sister Stamers had enjoyed a twenty-four hour stay in town with her mother, sister and relatives." The paper confirmed that "[o]n this occasion, she was accompanied by Nursing Sister Floyd, a Barnesville girl, whose sister is Mrs. Brown of King Street East." So, on this trip, Anna had the chance to visit her family in Moncton before travelling to Saint John and back to Halifax via Moncton. These visits would no doubt have been more meaningful because she and Nellie had travelled together and could discuss their experiences on their return trip to England.

The exact date of *Llandovery Castle*'s departure from Halifax is not clear. The Moncton *Daily Times* article on May 17 suggested the nursing sisters had left for Saint John shortly after arriving in Halifax. Based on this, they likely returned to Halifax on the nineteenth for departure on the twentieth or twenty-first. The passage was normally ten days. If the ship was in port for five days and left on May 20, it would have arrived in England on May 30 or 31.

On arrival in England Anna likely heard the devastating news from France that three of her nursing sister colleagues had been killed in an enemy air raid. The Germans had bombed No. 1 CGH on May 19, and within three days sixty-six patients and three Canadian nursing sisters were dead. On the day of the bombing, Katherine MacDonald of

Soldiers on the deck of *Llandovery Castle*, May 1918. At left in the third row is Private Shirley K. Taylor of Saint John, who survived the sinking on June 27, 1918.

Courtesy of Mary LeBlanc and Harold Wright

Brantford, Ontario, was the first Canadian nursing sister to die as a result of enemy action. Her colleagues Gladys Wake and Margaret Lowe died two days later of wounds. Anna and Margaret had worked together briefly at No. 16 CGH in Orpington in October and November 1917 before Margaret left for France.

Then, on May 30, 1918, the Germans bombed No. 3 Canadian Stationary Hospital. This time, two surgeons, sixteen orderlies, four patients, and three more Canadian nursing sisters died: Agnes MacPherson, Eden Pringle, and Dorothy Baldwin. Although Anna had not worked with them, still the news must have been shocking. Sadly, Anna — and everyone else — now knew that Germany considered hospitals fair targets whether on land or at sea.

Just before *Llandovery Castle*'s third and final trip to Canada, Nursing Sisters Margaret Fortescue, Gladys Sare, and Jessie McDirmaid joined the ship. Although they had worked at some of the same hospitals as Anna, she had not worked with them before. Margaret had served briefly

Canadian nursing sisters working among the ruins of No. 1 CGH
after a German bombing on May 19, 1918.

at No. 1 CGH, but only after Anna left for England. She had served at
No. 3 CGH, a casualty clearing station and, after falling ill, was assigned
to *Llandovery Castle*. Gladys had never been on the Continent, but had
served at Moore Barracks (later No. 11 CGH) before being transferred
to *Llandovery Castle* on June 4. Jessie had served in England and the
Mediterranean, and was assigned to *Llandovery Castle* on June 5, less than
a week before the ship left England for Halifax.

Llandovery Castle left Liverpool on June 10 and arrived in Halifax on
the seventeenth. On this third trip, the ship carried 644 military patients
for convalescence or discharge. Again, it is not clear exactly how long the
ship was in Halifax, but Anna must have decided that she did not have
enough time to make another visit home. Instead, as the *Evening Times
and Star* reported in July, "a fortnight ago today, she telephoned from
Halifax to her home while here just to say that she had arrived again, was

well and happy." The paper further reported that, "after a bit of shopping in the sister city, Miss Stamers re-joined the ship and sailed away on the fateful voyage on Thursday, the 19th." According to later reports, the ship sailed for Liverpool on the twentieth. Given the short time in port — just three days — it seems reasonable that Anna would have chosen to stay in Halifax, especially since each previous time she had made the trip to Canada, she had taken the opportunity to see her mother, siblings, and her Aunt Julia.

Other nursing sisters serving on board *Llandovery Castle* had family close to Halifax. Rena McLean was from Prince Edward Island, and Minnie Follette and Matron Fraser were from Nova Scotia. Rena, for reasons unknown, remained on board on all three trips and never took a trip home. On June 16, just before the final voyage, Rena wrote to her father. According to Katherine Dewar, Rena told him that she planned to ask for a transfer to France once she returned to England. She also told him that over half of the ship's soldiers were amputee cases. The others — from Quebec, Ontario, Saskatchewan, and British Columbia — could never make it home in the few days they had in port. Minnie Gallaher from

HMHS *Llandovery Castle* with hospital markings.
Courtesy of Harold Wright

Ottawa was unable to visit her family despite making three trips to Canada on *Llandovery Castle*. She had not seen them since she enlisted in 1915. According to later press reports, Minnie wrote to a friend expressing her disappointment that she had been unable to "take a run up to Ottawa for a day." Jean Templeman, also from Ottawa, had visited her family when on leave in 1917, but the same press reports said that, despite making three trips to Canada on *Llandovery Castle,* she never saw her father. Whether it was the unpredictability of the ship's schedule or the limited time in port, visits to and from parts west of the Maritime provinces were obviously more problematic.

On June 20, *Llandovery Castle* began the return voyage to Liverpool with 258 people aboard: Anna, along with thirteen of her fellow nursing sisters, eighty CAMC staff, and the ship's crew. The trip was without incident until the seventh night of the voyage, when, around 9:30 p.m., without any warning, a torpedo struck the ship. Within ten minutes, *Llandovery Castle* went down. Only twenty-four people survived. Anna and all her nursing colleagues were among the dead. The survivors alternated between sailing and paddling in their lifeboat until they were picked up by the destroyer HMS *Lysander* on Saturday, June 29.

Those who survived told their story to the press and later to a court. Sergeant Arthur Knight from London, Ontario, and Major Thomas Lyon from Vancouver were the principal witnesses who spoke about the circumstances after they were rescued. Two years later, Major Lyon testified at the trial of the first and second officers of U-86, Lieutenants Dithmar and Boldt, for violation of the laws and customs of war. The commander, Helmut Patzig, could not be apprehended and brought to trial, although he was convicted *in absentia*.

When the survivors told the full story of what happened that night, the reaction was horror. When the torpedo struck the ship, it destroyed the wireless and prevented the crew from sending a distress call. Although most of the ship's crew died when the torpedo struck the ship or when the engine exploded, the ship was equipped with enough lifeboats for all the passengers and crew. It was difficult to tell in the dark, but witnesses later testified that seven lifeboats made it safely into the sea, two on the port

Sergeant Arthur Knight.
Canada. Dept. of National Defence/
Library and Archives Canada/PA-007471

side of the ship (even-numbered boats) and five on the starboard side (odd-numbered boats). One of the lifeboats on the port side included Captain Sylvester and ten others, who began to pick up other men swimming in the sea.

Some members of the crew, the medical officers, the chaplain, and the nursing sisters managed to get into the lifeboats and tried to get away from the ship as it began to sink. Sergeant Knight was in Lifeboat No. 5, together with the fourteen nursing sisters. He described what happened: "Our boat was quickly loaded and lowered to the surface of the water. Then the crew of eight men and myself faced the difficulty of getting free from the ropes holding us to the ship's side. I broke two axes trying to cut ourselves away, but was unsuccessful. With the forward motion and choppy sea, the boat all the time was pounding against the ship's side." Knight explained why they were unable to manoeuvre the lifeboat: "To save the boat we tried to keep ourselves away by using the oars, and soon every one of the latter were broken. Finally, the ropes became loose at the top and we commenced to drift away." He praised the courage of the nurses in the face of certain death: "I estimate we were together in the boat about eight minutes. In that whole time, I did not hear a complaint or murmur from one of the sisters. There was not a cry for help or any outward evidence of fear."

As they drifted helplessly toward the stern of the ship, Matron Fraser turned to Knight and asked: "Sergeant, do you think there is any hope for us?"

I replied, "No," seeing myself our helplessness without oars and the sinking condition of the stern of the ship. A few seconds later we were drawn into the whirlpool of the submerged afterdeck, and the last I saw of the nursing sisters was as they were thrown over the side of the boat. All were wearing lifebelts, and of the fourteen two were in their nightdress, the others in uniform. It was doubtful if any of them came to the surface again, although I myself sank and came up three times. . . . We were carried towards the stern of the ship, when suddenly the Poop deck seemed to break away and sink. The suction drew us quickly into the vacuum, the boat tipped over sideways, and every occupant went under.

According to Knight, he managed to get away from the swirling waters surrounding the ship and hung onto a piece of debris until the captain's lifeboat came to his rescue.

After the initial chaos of getting off the ship, two of the five lifeboats on the starboard side capsized, leaving only three lifeboats on the starboard side and two on the port side still afloat. The captain's lifeboat was rescued on the morning of June 29 by *Lysander* after floating in the Atlantic for some thirty-six hours. The search for the other lifeboats continued. The British sloop *Snowdrop* and four American destroyers systematically searched the area where they thought the other boats might be. *Snowdrop* found one lifeboat, No. 6, about nine miles from the spot where *Lysander* rescued the survivors in the captain's boat. The search continued until July 1, but, although the weather was good, no other boats or survivors were found.

Another ship, HMS *Moreau*, did come across wreckage. Captain Kenneth Cummins described what he saw:

We were in the Bristol Channel, quite well out to sea, and suddenly we began going through corpses. The Germans had sunk a British hospital ship, the *Llandovery Castle*, and we were sailing through floating bodies. We were not allowed to stop—we just had to go straight through.... It was quite horrific, and my reaction was to vomit over the edge. It was something we could never have imagined... particularly the nurses: seeing these bodies of women and nurses, floating in the ocean, having been there some time. Huge aprons and skirts in billows, which looked almost like sails because they dried in the hot sun.

The sinking of *Llandovery Castle* received worldwide press coverage, attracting the attention of newspaper columnists and editors in Canada, the United States, Britain, and New Zealand. On July 2, Canada's *Globe* carried the story under the headline, "Hospital Ship, Plainly Marked, Sunk by Huns; *Llandovery Castle*, with Canadian Medicals." On the fifth, New Zealand's *Otago Daily Times* covered the story under the heading, "How Germany Makes War." On August 1, the *New York Times* published its account under the heading, "Sinking of the *Llandovery Castle*, Hospital Ship Deliberately Sunk by a German Submarine, With Heavy Loss of Life." The articles relied heavily on a statement containing first-hand accounts from the survivors issued by the British Admiralty. All accounts emphasized the terrible price paid by innocent non-combatants and the deliberate nature of the action. In the first week of July, the accounts given by Sergeant Knight and Major Lyon were reported in national newspapers across the world, revealing the full scope of German conduct.

On July 11, Knight was summoned to Buckingham Palace to offer his assessment of the facts to King George V. His account, originally published in the *Times*, was republished in the *Hospital* on July 13. Knight gave the reporter the same account that he had given to the King. He related that he had been "closely questioned by the King, especially as to what happened after the vessel was torpedoed" and, following his explanation, "his Majesty expressed his intense horror of the German outrage." In this account, Knight related that he had been taken aboard the submarine from his lifeboat, questioned, released and told to "get away quick." As Knight related it, he then saw the submarine "rushing

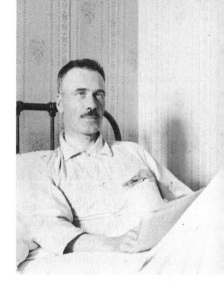

Major Thomas Lyon.
Canada. Dept. of National Defence/
Library and Archives Canada

about among the wreckage apparently trying to ram any other boat that might be afloat." Knight also reported that he heard heavy reports and some shells passed screaming over them. "I counted twenty shots and concluded that survivors in the water were being fired upon."

In fact, what troubled the King was what troubled the world. The sinking of *Llandovery Castle* was so shocking because victims who had managed to get into lifeboats were then deliberately rammed by the U-boat or "finished with shrapnel." Major Lyon, the Canadian surgeon who also survived, speculated on why the ship was targeted:

> The Germans seemed obsessed with the idea that American aviators were aboard, and it took us some time to convince them otherwise. Almost the first words they used when approaching our lifeboat were: "Where is the flying officer?" There were indeed plans for eight medical officers to make the voyage but at the last moment, the passage of one was cancelled. Evidently, the Germans had intelligence from a Halifax informant that eight officers were to be on board. However, they were not flying officers, they were medical officers.

Patzig, the submarine's commander, was not easily convinced. Lyon stated that the German commander ordered the lifeboat to come alongside. When they delayed while trying to rescue a man in the water, the commander shot over their heads with his revolver and made more threats. The Germans took Captain Sylvester, commander of *Llandovery*

Castle, and later Major Lyon aboard the submarine for questioning. According to Lyon, the Germans asked whether a wireless message had yet been sent requesting assistance. The Canadian officers assured him that there were no flying officers on board, only medical officers, and finally they were allowed to return to their lifeboat. According to Lyon, Patzig then turned away and "took his U-Boat on a smashing up cruise among the survivors and by hurling it hither and thither he succeeded in ramming and sinking all the boats and rafts except one (the master's boat) which escaped. The survivors in this boat heard the sound of gunfire behind them for some time."

Five days later, the British Admiralty provided a statement on the circumstances published in the *Times*. It confirmed that the ship had been torpedoed by an enemy submarine while displaying all regulation navigation and hospital lights and sank in about ten minutes. As the official statement read, "It is to be noted that in this — as indeed, in all other instances — the German submarine had a perfect right to stop and search the Hospital Ship under The Hague Convention. She preferred, however, to torpedo the *Llandovery Castle*." The report then provided details of events, including the accounts of Major Lyon, Sergeant Knight, and the other CAMC survivors. It included details given by another survivor, medical orderly Harry Hickman, of Saint John. Hickman stated that he also had been taken on board the submarine, questioned, and told to write the name of the ship in the U-boat logbook before being returned to the captain's boat.

On July 2, Andrew Bonar Law, Chancellor of the Exchequer, offered his thoughts in the British House of Commons on the sinking: "One would have thought that nothing new as regards German brutality could have happened, but the sinking of the *Llandovery Castle* was an unspeakable outrage." As for what actions might then be appropriate, Bonar Law was categorical: "The wild beast is at large. There is no use arguing or reasoning about it. The only thing to do is destroy. That is the duty and it is up to all the Allies to set their teeth until that end is achieved."

This kind of reaction was widespread. A writer in the *South African Nursing Record* commented: "The Hun has committed such revolting outrages that sometimes one wonders if one has any capacity for horror left; but an affair like the sinking of the hospital ship *Llandovery Castle* was so unspeakable as still to bring a gasp of surprise from all around the world." The reaction was proportionate to the crime. It was not just that *Llandovery Castle* had been deliberately torpedoed—by this point, it was the tenth British or Canadian hospital ship to be sunk by German torpedoes (HMHS *Warilda* was the last to be targeted, on August 3, 1918). Still, the loss of life on *Llandovery Castle* was the highest for any hospital ship deliberately targeted by the Germans in the war. More than that, however, the news coverage of the sinking focused on Patzig's actions and the first-hand accounts of survivors, not just the number of deaths. Andrew Macphail, official historian of the CAMC, says that the testimony of the survivors was incredible to those who were "not yet aware of the desperation into which the German military mind had sunk." The fact that lifeboats filled with survivors more than one hundred miles from land had been rammed and fired on by the German commander was a compelling story. The plight of the nursing sisters made it even more tragic. Macphail states: "the sacrifice of women profoundly moved the heart of the world."

The loss of *Llandovery Castle* brought about significant changes in naval practice. According to Macphail, "[w]hen sixteen hospital ships had been destroyed by submarines and mines, the melancholy conclusion was forced upon the Admiralty that the Red Cross and the Geneva Convention were no longer a protection from the enemy." Hospital ships now had their distinctive markings removed and they sailed as ordinary transports, armed to repel attack and supplied with a naval escort. "One achievement of the Germany Navy," Macphail says, "was to banish the Red Cross from the seas; the White and Red Ensign remained."

The sinking quickly became part of the Allies' propaganda war against Germany. The British contended, as the *Times* reported, that the Germans had a policy called *Spurlos Versenkt*—to sink without a trace—when a submarine torpedoed a ship. This claim was made based on testimony from survivors of the *Kildare* and *Westminster*, both sunk in the Mediterranean, "who attested to these facts"; the testimony of the

"Spurlos Versenkt," wartime propaganda poster.
Temple University Libraries, SCRC, Philadelphia, PA / PT 170095

survivors of *Llandovery Castle* added to the claim. After the sinking of *Llandovery Castle*, a poster was published with the banner *Spurlos Versenkt*, in German and an English translation. Below: "On June 27, 1918, the *Llandovery Castle* — a British hospital ship plainly marked with the Red Cross — was torpedoed by the Hun." The poster and the sordid story it represented was used to encourage Americans to buy more war bonds.

The sinking also hardened attitudes among Canadians toward Germans. On July 9, a Canadian newspaper reported on Prime Minister Borden's visit to the forces at the front. Afterwards, his "steely observation" was that "the sinking of the Canadian hospital ship *Llandovery Castle* will never be forgotten by our troops." For Canadians at home and at the front, the attack on the ship was murder.

Canadian soldiers on the Western Front had their first chance to avenge the deaths of their comrades at the Battle of Amiens in August. Two of the nursing sisters who died had connections to Saskatchewan, the home province of Brigadier George Tuxford, who commanded the 3rd Infantry Brigade. When issuing instructions to his troops, he added, "the battle cry on the 8th AUGUST should be '*Llandovery Castle*,' and that the cry should be the last thing to ring in the ears of the Hun as the bayonet is driven home." Canadian gunners wrote "Remember Llandovery Castle" in chalk on their shells before firing them. Officers urged their soldiers on, not just to defeat the Germans, but to seek retribution for the lives lost in *Llandovery Castle*. Historian Tim Cook also cites the frank recollections of Charles Yale Harrison, an American who served in the trenches with the CEF. In his novel, *Generals Die in Bed*, Harrison contends that the plight of those lost on *Llandovery Castle* motivated the soldiers to take no prisoners. According to this account, when the Germans were advancing, the British response was, "We do not heed. We are avenging the sinking of the hospital ship. We continue to fire." In fact, Harrison suggests this became accepted practice: "We say this on all sides. It has become an unofficial order. It is an understood thing." At the very least, the Germans' actions provided renewed motivation to fight on.

Once unleashed, righteous anger was hard to control. The stories were recounted, and resonated with the veterans, even if they did not form part of the official record. Cook argues that in the period immediately following the war there was no willingness to accept that British and Canadian troops had been motivated to seek retribution. Had that been admitted, it would have been difficult to maintain the moral high ground when presenting cases for consideration as war crimes. And the sinking of *Llandovery Castle* did become a precedent-setting case as one of the war crimes trials heard by the German Supreme Court, the *Reichsgericht*, at Leipzig.

The case could not proceed until 1920, after the Treaty of Versailles came into force. Claude Mullins later wrote about the Leipzig trials, explaining the delay: "It was then, and not till then, that the clauses of the Treaty, under which Military Tribunals were to try persons accused of having committed acts of violation against the Laws of Customs of War, could be brought into operation." Mullins pointed out that the selection of this case was significant, since there were many other examples of illegal actions against the French, Belgians, British, and Italians, and trying them all would destabilize the fragile German government. The Germans argued that evidence should be submitted to them, and that the Supreme Court of Leipzig would hear the case. *Llandovery Castle* was one of only six cases submitted by the British.

The case was finally heard in the summer of 1920, by which time Helmut Patzig, the commander of U-86, had moved to Danzig, and the German government lacked the jurisdiction to compel him to appear. However, his two subordinate officers, First Lieutenant and Adjutant Ludwig Dithmar and First Lieutenant and Merchant John Boldt were arrested and put on trial. Both refused to cooperate, stating that they had promised Patzig to be silent concerning the actions on the night of June 27, 1918. British and Canadian officers and members of the crew testified, as did crew of U-86 who were not charged. Second Officer Leslie Chapman, Fourth Officer A.J. Heather, and other survivors of *Llandovery Castle* gave evidence. Major Lyon was the only member of the CAMC who testified, presumably because he was the most senior surviving officer. In its Reasons for the Decision, the court cited evidence from Major Lyon, but Second Officer Leslie Chapman's testimony was particularly persuasive.

The focus of the proceedings was not on the torpedoing of *Llandovery Castle,* but rather on the actions of the U-boat commander and his officers after the ship had been sunk, with testimony confirming that U-86 had fired fourteen rounds from the 8.8 cm gun mounted on its stern. The court rendered its decision on July 16, 1921, finding that Patzig intended to sink the lifeboats, and that he "attained his object so far as only two of the boats were concerned." The court also pointed out that the survivors in those lifeboats could have been rescued on June 29, as was also the case for the captain's lifeboat, since the seas were calm. The court said: "The firing on the boats was an offence against the law of nations. In war on land the killing of unarmed enemies is not allowed... similarly in war at sea, the killing of shipwrecked people, who have taken refuge in lifeboats, is forbidden." Finally, "the act of Patzig is homicide according to para. 212 of the Penal Code. By sinking the lifeboats, he purposely killed the people who were in them."

Dithmar and Boldt were held to be accessories and sentenced to four years' imprisonment. The court reasoned that the two subordinates knew "that killing defenceless people in the lifeboats could be nothing else but a breach of the law. As naval officers by profession they were well aware... that one is not legally authorized to kill defenceless people." Although Dithmar and Boldt were jailed, their incarceration was short-lived. On November 22, 1921, the *Daily Telegraph and The Sun* reported that the two had escaped from prison. Although he was indicted *in absentia,* Patzig's conviction was quashed by the German courts in 1931 as part of two laws of amnesty. During the Second World War, Patzig served in uniform again from 1943 to 1945 as commander of a U-boat and then of the 26th U-boat Flotilla.

The Allies were disappointed with the results of the cases heard at Germany's *Reichsgericht,* both for the small number of cases finally presented and for their outcomes. The *Llandovery Castle* case, however, set a precedent that still has value a century later. As Jay Doucet, Gregory Haley, and Vivian McAllister argue, the findings against Dithmar and Boldt had a greater effect than the punishment meted out to them. They note that the court's ruling against Dithmar's claim that "he was only following orders" was used to reject similar claims made at the Nuremberg Trials following the Second World War. In addition, the establishment of the International Criminal Court grew out of the Leipzig trials and later the Nuremberg Trials. The authors also argue that today's Canadian Armed Forces draw on the findings of this case in teaching the principles in the Law of Armed Conflict. Put simply, they are taught, "It is wrong for a Canadian Armed Forces member to carry out an illegal order." Finally, and most directly relevant to Anna and her colleagues, and their families, "[t]his humane legacy may bring some solace to the relatives and descendants of the crew and the medical staff of HMHS *Llandovery Castle*, who routinely braved great peril while carrying out their noncombatant duties in the First World War."

How many people died in Patzig's post-sinking rampage was never determined. The number of victims was not the focus of the court's inquiry, but we do know that Anna and *Llandovery Castle*'s nursing sisters were not among them. In his statements to military officials and the press, Sergeant Knight said they were only in the lifeboat about eight minutes when it capsized. The nursing sisters were drowned in the vortex of swirling water created by the ship as it went down.

Chapter Eight

Honouring and Remembering

"She Hath Done What She Could..." —Mark 14:8

On July 4, 1918, one week after *Llandovery Castle* sank and all hope of finding more survivors was gone, Anna's mother, Lavinia, received a telegram from Ottawa. It confirmed that "Nursing sister Anna Irene Stamers rept miss bel [reported missing believed] drowned from *SS Llandovery Castle*." The telegram officially confirmed what was already in the newspapers that day. By then, an official letter of condolence from Matron-in-Chief Margaret Macdonald was already on its way. The letter began, "My dear Mrs. Stamers," and expressed both sympathy and outrage: "The Director of Medical Services asks me to extend to you and all members of your family our sincere sympathy and regret over the great loss sustained in the tragic death by drowning of Nursing Sister Stamers.... The abominable outrage in torpedoing a Hospital Ship is beyond mere words." She enclosed a copy of the account of one of the survivors, Major Lyons, and then continued on a more personal note: "Sister Stamers leaves behind an enviable record of faithful and devoted service. She was an example and inspiration to her juniors and her death is a distinct loss to the service in every way. It is some small comfort to recall that she spent a holiday with you less than a year ago." This touching letter served both to affirm the family's loss and to provide what official information was available to the family as quickly as possible. It

Funeral service for Nursing Sister Gladys Wake, who died of wounds
received in a German air raid on No. 1 CGH, May 19, 1918.

William Rider-Rider / Canada. Dept. of National Defence / Library and Archives Canada / PA-002562

says much about the depths of Lavinia's grief in those early days that she
had no recollection of receiving the telegram or the letter of condolence.
On January 1, 1919, she wrote to the Adjutant General, Canadian Militia,
stating that she had not received any official notice of her daughter's death
and only had confirmation from the newspapers.

Anna's death, and those of her colleagues, also had a significant effect
on her community, the country, and Canada's allies in the summer of
1918. All were united in their abhorrence of Germany's actions against
Llandovery Castle. By that time, Canadians had become hardened to the
deaths of soldiers in action. If the bodies were recovered, a simple service
was held, and they were buried along with other Canadian soldiers who

had died in service. This was also the case for the three nursing sisters killed by bombs at No. 1 CGH on May 19, 1918. Their nursing sister colleagues and other CAMC staff held a service for them, and they were buried alongside the soldiers. If local communities back in Canada held memorial services for these nurses, they did not receive much press coverage. On July 3, the Saint John *Daily Telegraph and the Sun* and Moncton *Daily Times* published a letter written by a Saint John native, W. Brindle, about the bombing and the deaths. Brindle praised the nursing sisters' courage, "the nurses quietly walked the ward from cot to cot, giving a drink to a thirsty one here, rearranging the pillows of a suffering one there, and with never a thought of danger, for they were miles and miles behind the lines and under the distinguishing mark of the Red Cross, most clearly showing in the moonlight, on every roof in the camp." The newspaper printed the article under the headline, "God Gives to Frail Women Serving in Bomb-Stricken Hospitals, Hearts of Men." In death, then, women who had been considered ministering angels of mercy were now lauded for their courage in the face of death, not just the comfort they provided.

News of *Llandovery Castle*'s fate travelled quickly to other nursing sisters. On July 6, Clare Gass wrote in her diary, "News of the sinking of our Canadian hospital ship *Llandovery Castle* reached us today. All the sisters are lost." Then, on the ninth, she wrote, "Miss Pearl Fraser, Miss Fortescue and Gladys Sare were all on board the hospital ship *Llandovery Castle*." On July 24, Anna's former matron, Mildred Forbes, wrote to her friend, "Wasn't it awful about those 14 girls on the hospital ship. I knew most of them and it haunts me at night. The Canadian girls have been paying the price lately."

As tragic as the bombing of No. 1 CGH had been, the sinking of *Llandovery Castle* captured the popular imagination for its wanton cruelty, drama, and the number of non-combatant deaths. Nursing sisters were not expected to die at the hands of the enemy, and certainly not by enemy action against a hospital ship. The sinking, therefore, received enormous press coverage in Canada, and Anna's memorial service was widely followed throughout New Brunswick. When Saint John held a memorial service for Anna, the *Daily Telegraph* reported the details on July 15 under the headline, "Impressive Tribute Paid to Memory of Martyred Nursing Sister Stamers." Anna had attended the former Brussels Street Baptist Church before it amalgamated with the Central Baptist Church, and the church invited the community to attend the service. It seems that Anna's death affected the citizens of Saint John, regardless of religious faith — according to the paper, a "very large number of people" attended from "many congregations and creeds." Also present were representatives of the Red Cross Society, a large body of active hospital nurses, the alumnae of the nursing society of New Brunswick, the Knights of Pythias, several returned soldiers in uniform, one military nurse, and a very large number of Anna's friends from throughout the city. The news coverage invoked the memory of another First World War nurse, Edith Cavell — who, while working in Belgium in 1915, was accused of treason and shot by a German firing squad — to explain the mood of the service. That evening, "The spirit of Edith Cavell which stirred the civilized world when she was brutally put to death by the Hun pervaded the Central Baptist Church." Anna's memorial service was not the first held in Saint John to pay tribute to one of its own killed on active service. But the reporter declared: "Although many impressive services have been held in the Loyalist city in the years since war was declared, that of last night seemed to produce a feeling more intense, more thoroughly in earnest, a keener demonstration of heart contact than any before."

The memorial service was opened by a mixed quartet and a prayer. The pastor then read the official government documents outlining the circumstances surrounding the sinking of *Llandovery Castle*. "From the very outbreak of the war, Germany's actions have evoked the condemnation of the world," Reverend D.J. MacPherson stated. "The sinking of the *Lusitania* was only an incident in a long succession of horrors. The torpedoing of the hospital ship the *Llandovery Castle* comes to us as a climax in a long list of atrocious ruthlessness." The pastor's remarks no doubt also reflected the views of the attendees. It was a righteous anger he invoked, and he was not wrong. The *Llandovery Castle* incident resulted in the greatest loss of life of any hospital ship in the war. Later, it would have the distinction of being the greatest disaster to that point in Canadian naval history.

The pastor then addressed Anna's death in the larger context of other victims of the war. He described the suffering of the people of Belgium and Poland, and the effects of the war on families and industry, declaring that the "astounding brutality of the Hun is an incredible revelation." But he was not yet done with his condemnation of the enemy. He captured the essence of the incident as related by the survivors:

> (1) that the crime was deliberately conceived (2) that it was unparalleled for calculated savagery (3) that ferocious efforts were made to obliterate all traces of the deed (4) that the only surviving lifeboat with its twenty-four occupants escaped almost by a hair's breadth, three attempts were made to sink it and one attempt to blow it to pieces (5) that the list of survivors includes only one officer and five of other ranks of the hospital personnel of ninety-eight (6) that all ranks, especially the fourteen Canadian nursing sisters who were lost, conducted themselves in the midst of events and incidents of the most terrifying character with a discipline impossible to excel (7) that the nurses who were lost had served months and some of them years in the danger zone in France again and again nursing German wounded (8) that these nurses not only had given water and medical aid to parched and bleeding enemy soldiers but had written down many dying statements by dying enemy soldiers and men and transmitted these through the Red Cross.

The effect of his statement was not just to describe Anna's untimely death, but also to contextualize it and commend Anna's service to both allied and enemy wounded.

Reverend MacPherson then described Anna's commitment to her faith, and said that "her sunny disposition, beautiful life and character, and keen clear intellect" were attributes that "eminently fitted her for the noble profession she had chosen." In talking about her term of service, he noted that Anna had "spent a year and one half in France ministering as an angel of mercy to the sick, wounded and dying soldier." He added that, in the words of one convalescing soldier, "She is like one's own true sister and has a heart as big as all out of doors." This description of Anna rings true: Matron Smith, her matron at No. 16 CGH, Orpington, had commented on Anna's kindness to the soldiers in her care. The pastor described her service on the hospital ship as "the more hazardous position which she so ably and nobly filled until her death on June 27." At the close of his remarks, he declared: "The memory of her life so nobly lived and given will be revered and cherished not only by those who knew her but what she hath done will be spoke as a memorial of her through the coming years."

Anna's young cousin George, son of her uncle C.J. Stamers, then unveiled a memorial to Anna and "stood at the salute while doing it." The memorial was an enlarged framed photograph of Anna in her working uniform. It was likely taken when she, Ethel, and Nellie were in Montreal together three years earlier, before sailing for England. Attached to the frame was a plate with the inscription: "In loving memory of Nursing Sister Anna Stamers, born at St. John (N.B.) January 15, 1888. While serving God, the nation and humanity, she came to her death in the sinking of the hospital ship *Llandovery Castle* by a German submarine, June 27, 1918. She hath done what she could." The latter part of the inscription would have been familiar to many attending the service—it was from the gospel of Mark, Chapter 14, verse 8.

Anna's role as a nurse brought tributes from the Red Cross Society of Canada, the Nurses Alumnae of the General Public Hospital, and the New Brunswick Association of Graduate Nurses. Her father's and uncle's connections might have been the link to the tributes from the Navy League of Canada, the Boy Scouts of Canada, and the Knights of Pythias. The family's long-standing connection to the Baptist Church, as well as Anna's own role in teaching Sunday School, brought floral tributes from the church's Board of Deacons, the infant class of the Sunday School, the Sunday School Superintendent, and its Willing Workers, Women's

Missionary Aid, and Baptist Youth. After the service concluded, there was an opportunity to offer condolences to the family.

Others in the congregation that day had also suffered their own loss when *Llandovery Castle* was sunk. Anna was one of twelve people from New Brunswick who died in the incident, five of them from Saint John. The mother of Kenneth Daley, a medical orderly on the ship, attended Anna's memorial service. As the newspaper reported it, Mrs. Daley, of Paradise Row, came forward to speak with Anna's mother, Lavinia. As she offered words of condolence, her voice shook with emotion when she shared that her own son, Kenneth, had also been a victim that day. Mrs. Daley then went on to tell Lavinia that, in addition to Kenneth, she had three other boys still in service in France.

Other New Brunswickers besides Daley were also lost. Albert Baker, Frederick Clark, William Clark, and Clement Scribner were all from Saint John, Robert Sanderson was from Woodstock, Frank Williams and David (Billy) Duffie came from Fredericton, and Edward MacPherson, Harry

"THEIR·NAME·LIVETH FOR·EVERMORE"

WILLIAM·MEEHAN AUG·16·1915	CHARLES·McCONAGHY JUNE·4·1918
CORP·WM·A·GORDON FEB·23·1916	EDWARD·M·MACPHERSON JUNE·27·1918
GEORGE·HOVEY MAY·21·1916	HARRY·HARRISON JUNE·27·1918
HARRY·DOYLE JUNE·2·1916	WALTER·B·SACRE JUNE·27·1918
GEORGE·A·FISHER SEPT·15·1916	MILTON·E·CLEGG AUG·9·1918
SERGT·FRED·WADE APRIL·9·1917	SERGT·HARRY·A·HERON SEPT·2·1918
CORP·WILLIAM·E·KAINE AUG·13·1917	H·WALLACE·CAMERON SEPT·2·1918
GEORGE·BALL OCT·30·1917	CORP·RONALD·C·ROBINSON SEPT·29·1918
JOHN·CHARNLEY ·1917·	J·CONLIN·POND OCT·28·1918
ROBERT·MORRIS ·1917·	CORP·HERBERT·L·MARKEY DEC·30·1918
LIEUT·JOHN·T·GIBSON FEB·10·1918	ALBERT·MORRIS ·1919·
JOHN·A·ROBINSON JAN·26·1921	

The names of Edward MacPherson, Harry Harrison, and Walter Sacre on the Marysville Cenotaph. Brent Wilson

Harrison, and Walter Sacre were from Marysville. All of these men were medical orderlies, classified not as officers like the nursing sisters but as "other ranks." The names of Sanderson, Williams, Duffie, MacPherson, Harrison, and Sacre were later inscribed on the cenotaphs in their hometowns, but those of the others are not on the Saint John Cenotaph.

Anna was not from an affluent family, but her family was active in the community. Perhaps the memory of her father was still a factor in the expressions of commemoration. From the floral tributes and number of organizations represented, clearly the religious community and service groups wanted to honour her service. It was both a tribute to her and a way to underscore the important work that her colleagues were still doing together with the Red Cross. Even if Canadians were struggling to maintain their active support for the war, it was not difficult to honour the humanitarian work of these nursing sisters. Later that week, the *Daily Telegraph and Sun* again reported on the effect of Anna's death on her extended family in Salisbury, New Brunswick. Under the headline, "Keen Sorrow for Sister Stamers," it noted that "they take a keen pride in her splendid career and realize that her name will go down in history as one of the splendid patriotic heroines of this great world war."

The same Sunday evening the service was held in Saint John, another service was under way in St. Andrew's Church in Toronto to commemorate those lost on *Llandovery Castle*. Two of the victims, Captain Arthur Vincent Leonard and Nursing Sister Mary Agnes McKenzie, were from Toronto, which might account for why a service was held there. The official program cites the date of their deaths as June 28, 1918, rather than June 27, an error which no doubt occurred in the rush to pay tribute to such a significant loss. The program lists Anna along with the thirteen other nursing sisters, the chaplain, and the three medical officers who drowned when *Llandovery Castle* sank. The service consisted of hymns, a reading of scripture, and a sermon by the Reverend Professor J.W. MacMillan. The *Toronto Globe* reported on the service under the headlines, "HEROIC NURSES ARE HONORED. 'Llandovery Castle' Memorial Service at New St. Andrew's. PROF. MACMILLAN SPEAKS. Dr. Eakin's Fine Tribute to Those Who Went Down With Ship." While the headline focused on the nursing sisters, the service celebrated the sacrifice of all on board—the sailors, the medical staff, and the nursing sisters. According to the report, "the front pews were occupied by nursing sisters in uniform, some of them wearing the little button signifying service overseas. The whole central part of the church was given up to nurses, of whom hundreds were present. A number of medical officers were there, too, and here and there one saw relatives of those in honour of whom the service was held." The report listed the names of all the medical officers and nursing sisters who died, and whereas the Saint John service focused on Anna exclusively, Reverend MacMillan told the congregants:

> There were on that vessel three classes. The sailors are men who have shown themselves most gallant souls. The torpedos have not frightened them from the ocean as the Germans foresaw. We would remember them tonight. The medical officers were in a profession which exemplifies what is worthiest in life today, the spirit of science, the spirit of obedience to law, the spirit of ministry. We would remember them tonight. And there stood beside these sailors and doctors and went down with them into the black water, nurses.

In his remarks, Reverend MacMillan did not differentiate between the physicians who held officer status and the medical orderlies who were privates and assisted the nursing sisters. Rather, MacMillan addressed the nursing sisters who were present and warned them not to take for granted the gains they had made as professionals during the war. According to the *Globe* article,

> It is commonly stated, he said, that this war is going to give woman her true position in the world. "Don't be too sure of it, my sisters," he warned. Reverend MacMillan then told the story of the Jews of Prague, who, breaking out of the Ghetto where they were confined, saved the city from an attack which was on the point of overwhelming it. The city

of Prague and the citizens presented them with a banner but still shut the gates of the Ghetto upon them at eventide. Be careful, the preacher said, that you aren't just given a banner and kept within the gate as before. See that this war wins a world victory for women.

The services in Saint John and Toronto were both organized by members of the faith community, recognizing the connection these victims had to their respective churches. They could be considered a substitute for a funeral service meant to help family and friends cope with the initial news of the death, provide the means for the community to honour their sacrifice, and mark their passing. It would be some time before any formal memorials were constructed by local or national organizations. And of course, the war was still ongoing.

In Macphail's official history of the CAMC, he lists all those members who "fell in the war or died while serving." He notes, "in the whole of the nursing service 17 were killed and 60 lost their lives at sea." The names of the officers and nursing sisters who died on *Llandovery Castle* are listed together with a brief reference to the incident. Anna's name is listed incorrectly as K.J. Stamers. The names of the "other ranks" are listed elsewhere, but the only means of linking them to the *Llandovery Castle* incident is through their date of death and the code "d, e.a." for died, enemy action. Anna is the only nursing sister from New Brunswick to be included in this Roll of Honour.

Exemplary service was recognized in several ways during the war. Soldiers and nursing sisters could be "mentioned in despatches" and, in the case of nursing sisters, they might receive the Royal Red Cross, 2nd Class, and later, if judged appropriate, the Royal Red Cross, 1st Class. Anna did not receive any commendation for her service while still alive, but after the war, her memory was preserved in various forms. Anna was not eligible for the 1914-15 Star because she had not served in France before December 31, 1915, but her mother received the bronze Memorial Plaque, paper Memorial Scroll, and the Memorial Cross. As Canada's Department of Veterans Affairs describes it, "The Memorial Cross (more often referred to as the Silver Cross) was first instituted... [on] December 1, 1919. It was awarded to mothers and widows (next of kin) of Canadian soldiers who died on active duty or whose death was consequently attributed to such duty." The Royal Canadian Legion note that "[t]he recipients, although not Veterans themselves, can wear the cross at any time. Each cross is engraved with the name, rank and service number of their child or spouse." There was no award ceremony; the Memorial Plaque and Scroll were sent to Lavinia on May 10, 1920, and the Memorial Cross followed on January 29, 1923. The whereabouts of Anna's memorials is unknown today.

Several postwar community initiatives were also undertaken to memorialize Anna's service and untimely death, primarily by nursing organizations. On November 11, 1920, the *Telegraph Journal* reported that a fund had been started by the Saint John School of Nursing for a memorial to honour the "heroic Nursing Sister Anna Stamers, of Saint John, who was sacrificed in the *Llandovery Castle* submarine crime." Although the initial effort began with a "tempting pantry sale," in her history of the Saint John General, Alberta Hanscome confirms that, by 1921, the Stamers Memorial Fund had raised over $600, a significant amount in that period.

On July 28, 1921, the *Daily Telegraph and The Sun* reported that a new nurses' home had opened and a tablet honouring Anna placed in the main corridor. Anna's mother, Lavinia, unveiled the tablet, which bore the inscription, "*In memory of Nursing Sister Anna Stamers who was lost on the Llandovery Castle.*" In this instance, another young Saint John nursing sister, Lenna May Jenner, was also honoured by having a room named after her. Lenna had died of natural causes in London a few months after she enlisted. As reported by the paper, in dedicating the room, her father, the Reverend J.H. Jenner, made several important observations. In recognizing that Anna had been one of a large group of nurses who offered their services to their country, he stated that he believed she was the only New Brunswick nurse to be killed on active service. He also stated that "it was well to recognize the loyalty and heroism of the girls who gave as devoted and patriotic service as the men." Reverend Jenner then recalled the tragic manner of Anna's death and assured all those in attendance that "the names of the nurses would live in memory" and "all who saw the tablet would be inspired by Miss Stamers's record."

Another memorial initiated by Anna's nursing colleagues was to establish a boy's ward in the new Saint John General Hospital with a fundraising goal of $1,200. In 1929, a "Bridge and Dance" event was held in the old hospital before its demolition, raising over $1,400 for the initiative. More than five hundred citizens turned out in support of the goal of establishing the ward as a memorial to "Heroic Nurse Anna Stamers." Most of Anna's colleagues were still in service at the time of her death, and this event would have been an opportunity for them to attend.

Although it had been more than a decade since Anna's death, the community needed to pay tribute, but also to move past the pain. On March 18, 1930, the *Evening Times-Globe* again recounted the story of Anna's death on *Llandovery Castle*, but, as the writer put it, "survivors of the war hesitate to hark back to the terrible days of the Great War, to stir up poignant griefs cabled into homes hour by hour." Just twelve years after the incident, there was already a concern that the memory might

fade. As the newspaper expressed it, "for the sake of a generation unborn at that time, such an example of sacrifice and patriotism as that of Nurse Anna Stamers, on such an occasion as tonight's, may well bear repetition as a highlighted inspiration." The writer recalled that the first memorial to Anna had been erected in the children's auditorium of the Central Baptist Church, just a few days after her death and, as a graduate of the Saint John General Hospital, her death was also memorialized in

Memorial headstone for Nursing Sister Anna Stamers, Fernhill Cemetery, Saint John, NB. Brent Wilson

In 2016, the IODE memorial at Fernhill Cemetery in Saint John was moved to make way for the Cross of Sacrifice installed by the Commonwealth War Graves Commission. Courtesy of Harold Wright

the front hall of the nurses' residence. The article stated: "it is the I.O.D.E. members' ideal that her memory shall be kept green in this her native province and that she shall have a place among those who in death are honored for their service to their country."

In 1936, the women of the Saint John IODE placed a headstone in Fernhill Cemetery, Saint John, in the soldiers' section known as the "Field of Honour." There is nothing in the IODE minutes or the records of the Fernhill Cemetery to indicate what prompted the marker to be placed there. This act of remembrance would be lost to history except for two articles in the Moncton *Daily Times* on June 25 and June 29. On the twenty-fifth, under the headline, "Mrs. A. E. Killam leaves today for Saint John to attend Ceremony honoring her niece who died in Sinking of *Llandovery Castle*," the paper reported that the headstone was "similar in size and design to those which mark the graves of ex-servicemen who have been laid to rest in that plot." Then, on the twenty-ninth, the paper ran a story under the headline, "Memory of Nursing Sister Stamers is honored at Saint John." It reported that "large numbers of the members of the I.O.D.E. gathered for the ceremony of unveiling the headstone to commemorate Nursing Sister Anna Stamers." The event was characterized as "one of quiet, impressive dignity." Anna's sister, Gladys (Mrs. John Addy), unveiled the stone, and Reverend Dr. Brice D. Knott paid tribute to Anna. Others present included Anna's uncle and aunt, Mr. and Mrs. C.J. Stamers, and her Aunt Julia, Mrs. A.E. Killam of Moncton, and Mr. A.H. Wetmore, the president of Fernhill Cemetery.

Eighty years later, in 2016, the Commonwealth War Graves Commission undertook a pilot project with six communities to foster commemoration of the war dead. Fernhill Cemetery in Saint John was one of the sites selected. When organizers discovered they needed to move the IODE memorial to Saint John's fallen to accommodate the installation of a Cross of Sacrifice, they contacted the IODE. About eighty-five people, including members of the IODE, attended the move, which took place on November 9. A local teacher and her students participated, with the students reading from their research on those being commemorated, including Anna Stamers. The event reignited interest in the wartime contributions of local veterans within the IODE and the local community.

Anna's church, Central Baptist Church, later merged with another, and the photograph on display in the children's auditorium disappeared. The Saint John General Hospital was demolished in 1995, and with it the ward named in Anna's honour. The only memorial still in place in New Brunswick to honour Anna's service and death is the headstone erected in Fernhill Cemetery by the IODE in 1936.

In November 1940, the Stewarton United Church in Ottawa erected a memorial to Anna's colleague, Jean Templeman. The *Ottawa Citizen* reported that "the only other Canadian nurse aboard was a young woman from New Brunswick who wore the blue and white of the nursing service," but did not cite her name. Sadly, unmentioned were the twelve other nurses who died along with Jean and her New Brunswick colleague.

Other communities honoured the memory of the nursing sisters of *Llandovery Castle*. On September 17, 1938, the Montreal *Gazette* reported that four trees had been planted by the IODE in memory of Edith Cavell, Alexina Dussault, Margaret Jane Fortescue, and Gladys Irene Sare, presumably because they were graduates of McGill University. In 1925, Matron Margaret Fraser was honoured by her community with the installation of a stained-glass window in the First Presbyterian Church in New Glasgow, Nova Scotia. Photographs of Matron Fraser and Colonel Thomas MacDonald, both Nova Scotians and graduates of Dalhousie University, were installed as memorials in the entrance hall of a medical research building in Halifax, built in 1924 with a donation by the Rockefeller and Carnegie foundations. The photographs had no inscription and, over time, the memory of who they were and why the photographs were placed there was lost. In the mid-1990s, when the building underwent refurbishment, the photos were taken down. Two surgeons who worked in the building inquired about their provenance and found out who they were. A 2018 article in the *Canadian Journal of Surgery* highlighted the story. The fact that those who initially installed the photos failed to include inscriptions and the circumstances of their deaths makes an important point, demonstrating that, while the medical community understood the importance of honouring the sacrifice, it failed to recognize that memory is fleeting. Ninety years later, no one knew who the honourees were or why their deaths were significant.

The British victims of *Llandovery Castle* are commemorated on the Tower Hill Memorial in London. The Canadian victims — including Anna and the forgotten medical orderlies — are listed on the Halifax Memorial to those lost at sea with no known grave, in Point Pleasant Park. Anna and her fellow nursing sisters are listed on Panel 2, commemorating those "whose lives were lost in the war and whose graves are at sea." The Halifax Military Heritage Preservation Society's website provides a history of the memorial, which was first established in 1924:

> The original memorial for those lost during the First World War was erected near the site of the present one at Point Pleasant in 1924. In 1956 that memorial was re-erected on the southern slope of Citadel Hill, with separate, detached panels added for the names of those lost in the Second World War. However, the memorial on Citadel Hill deteriorated to such an extent that it was deemed unworthy of its purpose; it was dismantled in 1966 and the eroded stone was consigned to Bedford Basin as the "Last Post" was sounded. The current memorial at Point Pleasant was unveiled in November 1967.

1918
NURSING SISTER
CAMPBELL C.
DOUGLAS C.J.
DUSSAULT A.
FOLLETTE M.A.
FORTESCUE M.J.
FRASER M.M.
GALLAHER M.K.
McDIARMID J.M.
McKENZIE M.A.
McLEAN R.M.
SAMPSON M.B.
SARE G.I.
STAMERS A.I.
TEMPLEMAN J.

(clockwise from top left):
Halifax Memorial to the Missing,
Point Pleasant Park, Halifax.
Panels of the Halifax Memorial:
with the names of those lost from
Llandovery Castle, and those of
the nursing sisters lost from
Llandovery Castle. Brent Wilson

The Canadian government also commemorated the work of the nursing sisters of the First World War. In January 1922, the Canadian Association of Trained Nurses, the forerunner of the Canadian Nurses Association, approached Prime Minister William Lyon Mackenzie King to gain his approval for the placement of a memorial in Parliament's new Centre Block. After much discussion, the prime minister, officials from Public Works, and the Nurses Association agreed on a design. The Curator of the House of Commons reports that the sculptor, George William Hill, created the piece from Italian marble. The monument's cost of $38,000 was covered by contributions from the nurses and their associations. The memorial is in the northern section of the Hall of Honour and remains the largest sculpture in Parliament's Centre Block.

According to the House of Commons curator, the prime minister's involvement resulted in a broadening of the memorial's meaning. Not just a memorial to the nursing sisters of the First World War, it became a "historical tableau" illustrating a wider period of Canadian history and experience, including a nurse in New France caring for an Indigenous child. As the curator explains, "while the classical allegorical style of the sculpture may require some interpretation, the inscription at the base of the monument is very clear":

> Erected by the nurses of Canada in remembrance of their sisters who gave their lives in the Great War, Nineteen Fourteen-Eighteen, and to perpetuate a noble tradition in relations of the old world and the new.
>
> Led by the Spirit of Humanity across the seas woman, by her tender ministrations to those in need, has given to the world the example of heroic service embracing three centuries of Canadian history.

When it was unveiled on August 24, 1926, more than eight hundred nurses attended the ceremony, which coincided with their annual meeting in Ottawa.

"The last parade" of Canadian nursing sisters, Parliament Hill, Ottawa, during the unveiling ceremony of the war memorial dedicated to them, August 24, 1926.

Library and Archives Canada / LAC-3604050

On May 21, 1939, King George VI unveiled the National War Memorial in Ottawa. Intended to honour those who fought in the First World War, it was called "The Response," to symbolize Canadians' willingness to serve not just Canada, but the larger Empire to which it belonged. Nursing sisters, as well as all others who served and died, were included in this monument. The bronze figures below the arch are "positioned in a hierarchical position, with a kilted infantryman with a machine gun, and a Lewis gunner, leading the way. Behind them are a pilot, an air mechanic, a sailor, a mounted dispatch rider, a member of the Canadian Cavalry Brigade, also on horseback, a pair of infantry rifleman, two nurses, a stretcher bearer..."

The hundredth anniversary of the First World War resulted in renewed interest in its stories, including the experiences of nursing sisters. In 2015, Historica Canada released a Heritage Minute depicting the German attack on No. 3 CSH at Doullens on May 29, 1918. It features Nursing Sister Eden Pringle, who was killed during the raid, and Nursing Sister Eleanor Thompson. Thompson was awarded the Military Medal for bravery during the attack for evacuating patients and extinguishing a fire caused by an overturned oil stove, despite being injured by a fallen beam. In fact, eight nursing sisters and a matron received the Military Medal for the courage they demonstrated during bombings and air raids in 1918. The Canadians recommended that the nursing sisters receive the Military Cross because of their courageous actions and because the award was specifically instituted for junior officers. The Commanding Officer of No. 1 CGH made the recommendation and it was supported by Canada's Director General Medical Services. The Canadians recommendation, however, was rejected by the British. British nursing sisters did not have a comparable rank, were not integrated into the military structure, and the British did not want to risk pressure from their nursing sisters for comparable treatment. Still, as Robert Fowler notes, "these nurses became the first Canadian women to win gallantry decorations... an exceptional recognition, so soon after suffragettes had been marching on the streets for women's rights and when military authorities had no vision that women would ever come under enemy fire." Canada's Heritage Minute helped to remind Canadians that nursing sisters not only served, but served bravely when the situation demanded it, just as their male colleagues did.

In June 2018, a memorial to the work of the professional and Voluntary Aid Detachment (VAD) nurses in the two world wars was erected in England. Work had been under way for six years "for a permanent monument to nurses." According to the BBC coverage of the unveiling, "It carries the names of nearly 1,300 nurses who died during or as a direct result of their service." A service of dedication was held for the monument at the National Memorial Arboretum in Alrewas, Staffordshire, attended by the Countess of Wessex. The website for the Nursing Memorial Appeal gives the history and purpose of the memorial. In the history section of the website an alphabetical Roll of Honour appears. Among those listed

Commemorative painting of the sinking of
Llandovery Castle by Silvia Pecota. Courtesy of Silvia Pecota Studio

is Anna Stamers, number 1074, age 30, with the date of her death on June 27, 1918.

Members of the Royal Medical Service held a commemorative event in Ottawa and Halifax on June 27, 2018, on the hundredth anniversary of the sinking of *Llandovery Castle*. Among the events was the unveiling of a commemorative painting of the sinking of the ship by artist Silvia Pecota.

Finally, in 2018, Canadian composer Stephanie Martin and librettist Paul Ciufo developed an opera to tell the story of *Llandovery Castle*. One hundred years later, it is the nursing sisters who are the focus, and the opera is described as "the stories of nurses who died in heroic service." According to the promotional material:

The opera focusses on the lives and service of 14 Canadian Nursing Sisters who died in the tragedy. The calm confidence, skill and selflessness of Canadian nurses during the Great War stand in stark contrast to the chaos and violence that surrounded them. From the horrors inflicted by inhuman trench warfare, the Sisters offered healing and compassion to soldiers on both sides of the conflict.

The story, dramatized for the audience, includes a focus on the lives of Matron Fraser and Nursing Sisters Rena McLean and Minnie Gallaher as characters, as well as two of the men who survived the sinking, Sergeant Knight and Major Lyon, and the German U-boat captain, Helmut Patzig. The composer of the opera, an organist at Toronto's Calvin Presbyterian Church, after working there for a decade had noticed a plaque on the church wall memorializing Mary Agnes McKenzie. When it finally caught her attention, it became the impetus for her work.

The sinking of *Llandovery Castle* had a great impact in June 1918, and for the next couple of decades the memorialization of those who died met a need in Canadian society. Memorializing gave meaning to the loss and brought into focus the opportunities that each might have had in life. Time tends to obscure the details, however, even of an event as tragic as this. The fact that the world faced another war with even greater catastrophic loss of life and appalling atrocities might have overshadowed the events of 1918. Now that we can so readily recall the events, we should also remember that, before they lost their lives, all those on board *Llandovery Castle* had served their country in war. Their service needs to be commemorated, not just their manner of death.

Chapter Nine

Coolness, Courage, and Skill

Anna was one of the more than 2,800 nursing sisters who served in the Canadian Army Medical Corps during the First World War, and one of the 2,504 who served overseas. She chose, as did all Canadian nursing sisters in the Great War, to serve willingly and eagerly. Desmond Morton writes: "Wars are made by masses of people, and masses are made up of individuals, with their own motives and experiences, joys, terrors and tragedies." Anna's story, while tragic, allows us to understand the experience of Canadian nurses through the details of one woman's service. As Christine Hallett notes, "[t]he hitherto neglected writings of First World War nurses cast light on the nature of the suffering endured by combatants and on the realities of what they experienced."

Following the war, Sir Andrew Macphail wrote the official history of the CAMC. He had expected that Matron Macdonald would write a full account of the work of the nursing sisters, which did not transpire. Macphail wrote briefly of the nurses' experiences and how difficult it was for those who faced this challenge day after day, year after year: "To witness this suffering which they could so imperfectly allay was the continuous and appalling experience of the nurses at the front and at the base." At the beginning of the war, Colonel Guy Carlton Jones, Director-General of the CAMC, had cautioned the applicants that military nursing was not like civilian nursing. Military life, he warned them, would be difficult, and many of them simply would not be suited for it. They would need "coolness, courage and skill." Precisely how he differentiated coolness from courage is not clear. The only way to know if one possessed these qualities was to serve in "the crucible of war." Even though they signed up for the duration of the war, none expected that the war would continue for four long years. Still hopeful, Clare Gass wrote in her diary, on the last day of December 1916, "surely this will be the year that the war will end." During the great battles on the Western Front, the incoming wounded taxed the physical and emotional strength of the nurses themselves and almost overwhelmed their ability to care for the soldiers. Yet, even when the war seemed to be never-ending, the nursing sisters showed they had another important attribute: resilience, the capacity to endure.

Although Anna had only two years of private nursing experience before signing up, her earlier life as the child of a single mother and her age — at twenty-seven when she was taken on strength — meant she had the maturity, the "coolness," that was required. Christine Hallett argues that the trained nurses, unlike the volunteers, had encountered trauma before, and "like the 'old contemptibles' of the BEF, the trained nurses had some inkling of what to expect, and were able to cope with the horror and hold a nursing service together throughout the war." One of the most important qualities for a military nurse, Hallett says, was the ability to show leadership to junior staff. Anna's service file does not state whether she was a ward nurse or a surgical nurse or if she had a supervisory role. In her letter of condolence to Anna's mother, however, Matron Macdonald assured Lavinia that Anna was an example to the junior nurses.

As Anna's record demonstrates, working as a nurse in the First World War was a dangerous pursuit, and exposure to the work itself for sustained periods was difficult. As Hallett points out, the very act of military nursing exposed these women to trauma on an unimaginable scale. Wounds from shrapnel and gas were often horrific, and the inability to control infection effectively meant that even gunshot wounds were often fatal. Most nurses were able to withstand exposure to these conditions for a limited time. Many expressed how driven they felt—unable to rest or take time for themselves because their patients could not do so. And some drove themselves beyond the limits of their endurance.

Yet most of the nursing sisters were stoic and seemed able to take what joys and sorrows came their way, despite the carnage. For some, a rest would be enough to rejuvenate them; others became no longer able to function effectively, were hospitalized, and had to resign. All the nurses worked long periods without reasonable rest—in this respect, they were no different than the soldiers. Perhaps the example of the stoicism of the soldiers was one reason the nursing sisters felt that they had to carry on. Hallett remarks on the stoicism of the nurses: "the 'stiff upper lip' of Edwardian British and Dominion society that dominated and determined their behaviour." She notes that, whereas later societies might view this phlegmatic response as repressive, it was part of the cultural fabric of the era, and both patients and nursing sisters assumed this persona as a coping mechanism and as a means of enabling healing to take place.

Despite the exhausting work and exposure to illness, Anna had only two periods of sickness during the three years she served. The first was for an ear infection in June 1916, when she was adapting to life in hutments in France. When she recovered, she carried on through one of the most demanding periods of that year. Then, after a two-week leave and return to No. 1 CGH, she worked without a break until mid-May 1917, through the intense demands following the Battle of Arras, of which Vimy Ridge was a part. When she was struck off strength at No. 1 CGH and transferred to England, she was clearly in need of an extended rest. After she had had the opportunity to rest and re-energize, she remained in England and served for a further six months. Had she not perished on *Llandovery Castle*, there is every indication that she would have continued to serve out her time for the duration of the war.

During her service in England and France Anna did what all the nurses set out to do: care for the wounded. Taking time to listen to the patient was critical. Hallett argues that nurses helped soldiers recover by listening to their outrageous experiences. In Anna's performance appraisal just a few months before her death, Matron Smith alluded to her focus on patient care rather than on administrative tasks. Anna, she stated, "was very good to the patients but did not keep a very tidy ward." Hallett quotes another nursing sister, Edna Pengelly, from New Zealand, who took the same approach: "Today I have actually sat and held a patient's hand and stroked his brow, and he seemed calmed and quietened by the proceeding." Hallett identifies three important elements to a nurse's work: "her technical proficiency, which was formed through years of training, her practice wisdom and awareness, which developed through carefully supervised experience; and her adoption of a particular persona." But this persona, this composure, was sometimes difficult to sustain: "The woman who nursed the wounded of the First World War was a person who combined moral strength with compassion...nursing was, above all, synonymous with kindness and the nurse's reputation for kindness made her a vital asset to the war office. The morale of combatants was sustained, in part, because of the belief that if wounded, they would be well cared for." And, as their visits back home demonstrated, this belief was also of great comfort to the soldiers' families.

Hallett nevertheless states that "[i]t is impossible to quantify nursing work in terms of clearly demonstrable outcomes. The inability to measure its successes has always been the nemesis of the nursing profession. How does one count and tabulate pressure sores that never developed or wound infections that never happened?" As Susan Mann relates, "the nurses brought lads back from the brink of madness and accompanied them to the edge of death....The nurses did all this, year after year, day and night, the rhythm of their work regulated by the ebb and flow from battle." Hallett writes, "these achievements depended to a great extent on the care, quick thinking and attention to detail of nurses."

Throughout her three years of service, Anna was part of the Canadian contingent that provided this care and could take pride in those achievements. As Hallett writes, "nurses saw themselves as fighting against pain, disease and death. Theirs was the 'second battlefield' where the wounded were drawn back from the abyss of death and by inhabiting that battlefield, nurses themselves faced hardship, injury and sometimes death." These nursing sisters confronted the human suffering of war on a scale never seen before. Yet, as Cynthia Toman argues, the nursing sisters felt fulfilled by a sense of purpose. Nursing Sister Luella Denton, from Ontario, wrote to a friend: "I also realized that it has been a great privilege coming over here...I have seen some of the big things of life. I've been with so many souls as they crossed the border and then one knows what counts...I've seen both our own splendid men and the enemy suffer—all human beings and no difference then." Like Luella, Anna confronted the effects of hideous injuries, and nursed men who would be maimed for life. She would have lost many of her patients and, like her colleagues, come to the realization that, despite her best care, death was sometimes a more merciful outcome.

One of the defining characteristics of the nursing sisters who served in the First World War was their ability to adapt and demonstrate flexibility. They developed many skills and proved they were equal to the challenge. Yet, once peace came and the threat of war had passed, real change was slow. The nurses had developed extensive experience, demonstrated courage and strength, even gained a new-found status as voters. But although the process of change for women had begun, its benefits were elusive. The profession of nursing had gained legitimacy, but, for many, the increase in enrolment meant that postwar opportunities were few.

In 1921, Matron Macdonald wrote a report that, while succinct, encapsulated the work of Anna and the nursing sisters:

> Arduous duties were carried on under most trying conditions, and many were the discomforts endured, yet always the sisters adapted themselves to overcome, as far as possible, whatever difficulties presented....In periods of gravest danger they were superb....During enemy bombardment in France and England, and at the sinking of the Hospital Ship *Llandovery Castle*, the courage displayed by the Nursing Staff matched that of the greatest heroes of the war.

During their service, Anna and her nursing sister colleagues demonstrated that courage was not just a male characteristic but a human one.

Witnesses lauded the bravery of all the nursing sisters from *Llandovery Castle* as they faced their terrible plight that night in June 1918. Anna's body and those of her thirteen colleagues remain at sea, where they are "asleep in the deep," as Matron MacLatchy of No. 3 CGH so poignantly expressed it. The manner in which Anna and her colleagues died had far-reaching effects. Immediately thereafter, it hardened attitudes toward the enemy and gave new impetus to the soldiers and indeed to the country to carry on. But it also demonstrated that killing humanitarian workers, even when under a direct order, is never justified. That legal precedent is a lasting legacy.

In August 1914, the war had barely begun when the British suffered their first devastating losses at the Battle of Mons. After the deaths of many of his friends a month later at the First Battle of the Marne, Lawrence Binyon wrote a poem, "For the Fallen," a portion of which is now recited by millions at memorial services on Remembrance Day:

> They shall not grow old, as we that are left grow old:
> Age shall not weary them, nor the years condemn.
> At the going down of the sun and in the morning
> We will remember them.

In the retelling of Anna's wartime experiences that she and her nursing sister colleagues faced, we pay tribute to their service and sacrifice. It is the least we can do.

Appendix

New Brunswick Nursing Sisters Who Served with the Canadian Army Medical Corps in the First World War

The 165 nursing sisters listed in the following table had a New Brunswick connection as identified in online sources, newspapers, texts, and the website Canadian Great War Project (http://www.canadiangreat warproject.com). Twelve nursing sisters received the Royal Red Cross and three others received special commendation. The majority of the nursing sisters signed up between 1915 and 1918. Six were taken on strength in 1914, 36 in 1915, 39 in 1916, 47 in 1917, 34 in 1918, and finally 3 in 1919.

Of the 165 nursing sisters listed, 128 were born in New Brunswick or their service file shows that they had (1) next of kin in New Brunswick or (2) were taken on strength in New Brunswick. The 37 others were born in New Brunswick but there is no other information linking them to the province in their service file. In three instances, the nursing sisters were not born in New Brunswick but were living there at the time they did their attestation.

According to Andrew Macphail, when the Canadian universities organized medical units, three US universities also did so: Harvard, Chicago, and Western Reserve. Of the 165 nursing sisters listed here, 15 served with the Harvard Medical Unit before being taken on strength with the CAMC. Two nursing sisters served with QAIMNS before being taken on strength with the CAMC.

Although there might have been others, the 12 nursing sisters identified with an asterisk served at No. 1 CGH, France, the same hospital where Anna Stamers served for the longest in her career.

Abbreviations

CAMC   Canadian Army Medical Corps

LAC   Library and Archives Canada

NOK   Next of kin

PA   Present address (when taken on strength)

QAIMNS   Queen Alexandra's Imperial Military Nursing Service

RRC   Royal Red Cross, 1st class or 2nd class

School   School of Nursing, graduation year when known

SJSN   Saint John School of Nursing

TOS   Taken on strength

Name	Birthplace	Year Born	Attestation Date	LAC File: Comments	School
Anderson, Martha Jane	Royal Road	1881	Feb 17, 1917	B0161-S065	
Armstrong, Florence Mary*	Campbellton	1888	Feb 4, 1915	B0227-S004	SJSN 1911
Armstrong, Muriel	Hopewell Cape, NOK Niagara-on-the-Lake, ON	1890	Feb 24, 1915	B0234-S004	
Babbitt, Elizabeth	Fredericton	1880	Jun 20, 1918	B0324-S019	
Babbitt, Ella Pearl	Gagetown	1883	Apr 13, 1915	B0324-S017	McGill
Baker, Gertrude	Caribou, ME, NOK Moncton	1880	Apr 6, 1916	B0370-S034 Harvard, 9 months	
Balloch, Pauline D.	Centreville	1882	May 2, 1917	B0400-S040	
Barnhill, Mary Elizabeth	Fairville	1887	Aug 6, 1916	B0455-S013	SJSN 1914

Name	Birthplace	Year Born	Attestation Date	LAC File: Comments	School
Barry, Emma Ella	Melrose	1888	Apr 3, 1916	B0474-S002	SJSN 1911
Barton, Irene Maude	Pine Ridge	1892	Jun 3, 1915	B0488-S020	
Baskin, Eliza Margaret	Saint John, NOK Ottawa	1892	Dec 23, 1916	B0493-S012	
Baxter, Sarah Louise	Saint John, NOK Toronto	1891	Jan 17, 1917	B0521-S008 TOS London	
Beach, Margaret	Meadows	1892	Jun 24, 1918	B0529-S051 QAIMNS, 18 months	
Bell, Ethel G.	Taymouth	1888	Feb 12, 1917	B0611-S003	
Boyer, Ethel L.	Hartland	1883	Sep 16, 1915	B0979-S070	
Brittain, Elizabeth	Saint John	1890	Jun 12, 1917	B1079-S011	SJSN 1915
Brown, Katharine	Woodstock	1881	May 9, 1917	B1166-S035	
Burns, Ada Aldane	Saint John	1875	Jun 20, 1918	B1298-S009	SJSN 1897
Burns, Alberta L.	Saint John	1883	Aug 21, 1916	B1298-S015	
Burns, Georgina Louise	Bathurst, NOK London, UK	1879	Mar 17, 1917	B1301-S044 TOS England	
Burns, Laura Bell	Saint John	1881	Jan 4, 1917	B1305-S025	
Burpee, Eleanor Bell	Waterville, NOK Vancouver	1879	Sep 28, 1914	B1310-S030 RRC 2nd class	
Calhoun, Sara Ellis	United States, NOK Saint John	1893	Mar 27, 1917	B-1389-5011	
Cambridge, Ella Sarah	Gibson	1885	Mar 27, 1917	B1398-S018	SJSN 1914

Name	Birthplace	Year Born	Attestation Date	LAC File: Comments	School
Campbell, Marguerita Chalmers Montgomery	Sussex	1891	Jan 29, 1917	B6306-S019	
Casswell, Edith Jervis	Gagetown	1890	Jan 25, 1916	B1571-S026	McGill
Clancy, Mary	Newcastle	1888	Apr 12, 1918	B1717-S053 Harvard, 12 months	
Clinch, Mildred	Wisconsin, NOK Chamcook	1893	Jul 8, 1918	B1802-S039 Harvard, 21 months	
Colter, Bessie Long	Keswick	1874	Dec 24, 1916	B1891-S027	
Compton, Musetta	Fairville	1894	Dec 18, 1916	B1902-S046	SJSN 1916
Condon, Marguerite	Moncton, NOK Halifax	1889	Jun 10, 1916	B1905-S039 Harvard, ? months	
Crawford, Margaret C.	Saint John	1892	Nov 19, 1919	B2123-S054 CAMC 24 months	
Creaghan, Aileen	Newcastle	1887	Apr 3, 1916	B2128-S015	
Davies, Margaret	England, NOK Nova Scotia	1889	Apr 3, 1917	B2352-S012 PA Saint John	SJSN 1914
Dawson, Laura Annie	Hillsboro	1892	Jan 25, 1917	B2372-S021	
Day, Edna	Trenton, ON, NOK Moncton	1889	Jun 17, 1918	B2377-S005 QAIMNS, 9 months	
Delaney, Ethel Mary	Saint John	1887	Jun 20, 1918	B2415-S037	

Name	Birthplace	Year Born	Attestation Date	LAC File: Comments	School
Desbrisay, Ella	New Mills, NOK Vancouver	1864	Feb 1, 1919	B2460-S055	
Dewar, Evaline Jane	Michigan, NOK Campbellton	1888	Sep 26, 1917	B2492-S054	
Dibblee, Margaret Neil	Woodstock	1887	Oct 16, 1915	B5059-S048	
Dickie, Elizabeth L.	River Charlo	1883	Apr 13, 1915	B2507-S055	McGill
Dickson, Edna Leah	Hammond River	1884	Feb 8, 1917	B2537-S007	
Doherty, Mary Helen	Campbellton	1892	Jul 20, 1916	B2567-S026	
Domville, Mary Lucretia*	Saint John, NOK Montreal	1881	Jan 22, 1915	B2577-S002	
Donnelly, Agnes Eva	Jacquet River	1892	Sep 9, 1916	B2591-S029	
Donohue, Nellie*	Saint John	1885	May 12, 1915	B2579-S044	SJSN 1913
Dooe, Clara	St. Stephen	1882	Aug 16, 1916	B2599-S031	
Draffin, Isobel	Ontario, NOK Rothesay	1878	Feb 2, 1916	B2656-S009 PA New Brunswick	
Dunham, Margaret Ponsford	West Saint John	1887	Aug 16, 1916	B2740-S007	
Dykeman, Huilota	Nova Scotia, NOK Saint John	1893	Jul 4, 1918	B2791-S044	
Ellis, Margaret M.*	Bathurst	1878	Feb 6, 1915	B2886-S024	
Estabrook, Hannah	Saint John	1880	Jan 25, 1917	B2932-S008 Harvard, 9 months	

Name	Birthplace	Year Born	Attestation Date	LAC File: Comments	School
Everett, Pearl Allison	Saint John, NOK Medford, MA	1885	Apr 7, 1916	B2958-S056 Harvard, 9 months	
Fear, Florence Morgan	Springhill Mines, NS	1891	Nov 2, 1916	B3020-S006 PA Saint John	SJSN 1914
Fearon, Margaret Isabel	Bass River	1888	Jun 3, 1915	B3021-S009 RRC 2nd class	
Fenton, Margaret	Chatham, NOK Saskatchewan	1883	Apr 17, 1917	B3036-S025 Medaille d'Honneur	
Fessenden, Edith Juanita	Montreal	1890	Jul 4, 1918	B3065-S035 PA Fredericton	
Fisher, Alice Chipman	Chatham	1889	Jul 5, 1918	B3102-S048	
Floyd, Nellie*	Titusville	1887	Jun 3, 1915	B3159-S030	SJSN 1910
Forgey, Bertha*	Saint John	1882	Apr 16, 1915	B3201-S061	McGill
Foss, Nora Gleeson	Fairville	1887	Dec 2, 1916	B3224-S025	SJSN 1907
Foster, Georgie Perkins	Saint John	1881	Jan 6, 1917	B3229-S039	
Fox, Pearl Hazelton	Lower Gagetown	1892	Mar 27, 1917	B3255-S032	SJSN 1916
Fraser, Florence	Flatlands, NOK Matapedia, QC	1892	Aug 2, 1918	B3279-S045	
Gamblin, Anna Pearl	Sussex	1892	Jun 10, 1916	B3392-S003	
Gamblin, Jeanne Elizabeth	Sussex	1890	Jul 4, 1918	B3392-S007	

Name	Birthplace	Year Born	Attestation Date	LAC File: Comments	School
Gardiner, Catherine Finley	Hibernia, Queens County	1886	Jan 26, 1917	B3403-S030	
Gaskin, Bessie Eunice	Saint John	1889	Apr 1, 1916	B3435-S032	SJSN 1910
Gaskin, Maude Pearl	Saint John	1887	Sep 1, 1916	B3435-S043	SJSN 1907
Gerow, Clara Evelyn	Saint John	1878	Apr 6, 1917	B3481A-S004	
Gillis, Lowella Louisa*	Tide Head	1884	Apr 22, 1915	B3550-S030	McGill
Gleeson, Helen	Saint John, NOK Ottawa	1892	Nov 8, 1915	B3581-S055	
Glendenning, Margaret V.	Canobie	1893	Jun 10, 1918	B3583-S023	
Godin, Alma	Grantham	1888	Nov 8, 1915	B3692-S020	
Graham, Ruby Rutherford	Campbellton	1890	Apr 22, 1915	B3711-S018	McGill
Granville, Edna May	Saint John	1882	May 31, 1918	B3740-S017	
Gratton, Rose Anna	Moncton, NOK Pictou, NS	1887	Sep 24, 1914	B3472-S063	
Greene, Della Margaret	Moncton, NOK United States	1894	Nov 14, 1918	B3772-S037	
Gregory, Lyla Hattie	Saint John	1888	May 11, 1917	B3810-S055	
Gremley, Elizabeth Scott	Newcastle	1892	Nov 23, 1917	B3815-S045	
Hare, Catherine Margaret	Saint John	1876	Sep 25, 1914	B4053-S035 RRC 2nd class	

Name	Birthplace	Year Born	Attestation Date	LAC File: Comments	School
Harper, Grace Elizabeth	Jacksonville	1895	Mar 17, 1917	B4070-S032	
Hatheway, Elsie Robertson	Saint John	1892	Jul 7, 1917	B4154-S039	
Hegan, Alice Parker	Saint John	1877	Nov 9, 1918	B4232-S038	
Hegan, Edith Tilley (Matron)	Saint John	1881	Feb 4, 1915	B4232-S040 RRC 1st class	
Hibbard, Alice Laura	St. George	1888	Apr 4, 1917	B4315-S022	
Hocken, Florence Mary	Moncton, NOK Newfoundland	1886	Jun 10, 1916	B4402-S044 Harvard, 6 months	
Howard, Mary Munroe	Grand Falls, NOK Fort Kent, ME	1887	Jun 25, 1918	B4543-S019 PA Halifax	
Hudson, Jewel Gladys	Richibucto	1886	Apr 7, 1916	B4578-S014 Harvard, 5 months	
Hughes, Isabel Crandell*	Moncton, NOK England	1886	Sep 2, 1915	B4592-S041	
Humble, Emma Hortense	Stanley	1886	Sep 11, 1916	B4607-S032 Harvard, 15 months	
Ingraham, Idella May	New Brunswick, NOK Massachusetts	1881	Apr 16, 1918	B4694-S031 PA Montreal	
Jamieson, Mabelle Clara*	Campbellton	1891	Sep 26, 1914	B4784-S043 RRC 2nd class	
Jenner, Lenna Mae	Brookfield	1889	Jun 25, 1918	B4821-S012	

Name	Birthplace	Year Born	Attestation Date	LAC File: Comments	School
Kerr, Edith Sarah Mignon	Saint John	1888	Jun 27, 1918	B5115-S015	
King, Elizabeth Churchill	Jacksonville	1886	Apr 2, 1917	B5162-S004	
King, Nellie	Grand Falls	1889	Apr 3, 1916	B5174-S002	
Kingston, Ruth	Moncton	1892	Apr 1, 1916	B5185-S019	
Knight, Kathleen	Moncton	1888	Apr 4, 1916	B5228-S018	Laval
Leishman, Jean Campbell	Chatham, NOK Ontario	1882	Jun 12, 1919	B5559-S011	
Lewin, Mabel Eliza	Benton	1876	Jul 27, 1917	B5615-S036 Harvard, 11 months	
Lockhart, Ina Laura	Petitcodiac	1889	Jul 31, 1917	B5705-S001 Harvard, 6 months	
Loggie, Ruth	Burnt Church	1883	Apr 13, 1915	B5717-S028	McGill
MacDonald, Jessie Belle	Bathurst	1890	Oct 28, 1915	B6735-S025	
MacDonald, Nellie*	Chatham	1883	May 12, 1915	B6755-S015	SJSN 1907
MacKeen, Frances	Glace Bay, NS, NOK Rothesay	1889	Apr 18, 1915	B6941-S043	McGill
MacKenzie, Florence H.	Moncton	1885	May 5, 1917	B6968-S040	
Mackintosh, Olive Janet	Dublin	1893	Jan 27, 1917	B6899-S004	SJSN 1916
MacLellan, Milla	Campbellton	1890	Feb 28, 1918	B7063-S016	
MacRoberts, Edith Louise	Saint John	1890	Apr 28, 1917	B7208-S024	

Name	Birthplace	Year Born	Attestation Date	LAC File: Comments	School
Mallory, Charlotte E.	Saint John, NOK Calgary	1888	Feb 28, 1915	B5874-S009	
Maxwell, Marion Crawford	Saint John	1891	May 29, 1917	B6064-S040 QAIMNS, 12 months	
McAffee, Minnie	Woodstock	1880	May 12, 1915	B6563-S005 RRC 1st class	
McAlpine, Lillian Hazen	Upper Hampstead	1884	Jan 9, 1917	B6569-S025	
McAnn, Jennie May	Moncton	1890	Jul 15, 1917	B6614-S010	
McCafferty, Edith (Matron)*	Saint John	1877	May 12, 1915	B6600-S021 RRC 1st class	
McInerney, Ellen (Matron)	Richibucto	1888	Dec 26, 1916	B6881-S037 Medaille d'Honneur	
McIntyre, Annie Enid	Springfield	1894	May 1, 1917	B6902-S040	
McKay, Ruth Esther	Moncton	1891	Mar 13, 1917	B6937-S003	
McKenzie, Georgia Etta	Norton, NOK Massachusetts	1880	Mar 9, 1916	B6970-S029 Joint War Commission	
McKiel, Theodora	Bathurst	1869	Sep 24, 1914	B6991-S026 RRC 2nd class	
McManus, Lisa Theresa	Memramcook, NOK Nova Scotia	1889	Jul 26, 1918	B7103-S019	
Moody, Ethel*	Titusville	1879	Jun 3, 1915	B6310-S011	SJSN 1911
Murphy, May Veronica	Woodstock	1880	Sep 19, 1918	B6515-S029	

Name	Birthplace	Year Born	Attestation Date	LAC File: Comments	School
Newlands, Jean Watson	Michigan, NOK Saint John	1890	Jul 26, 1916	B7291-S006	
Orr, Mary Maltby	Newcastle	1882	May 12, 1915	B7488-S076	
Parks, Margaret (Dr.)*	Saint John	1876	Sep 28, 1914	B6703-S010 RRC 2nd class	McGill
Patterson, Edith Derling	Saint John	1896	Feb 26, 1918	B7638-S011	
Peters, Julia	Apohaqui	1889	Jul 7, 1918	B7761-S012	SJSN 1914
Powers, Alice	Saint John	1884	Apr 14, 1915	B7947-S030	SJSN 1906
Pratt Patterson, Margaret	Queens County, NOK California	1881	Dec 20, 1917	B7957-S006 TOS Toronto	
Rawlins, Inez Dayton	Saint John, NOK Manitoba	1882	Oct 30, 1917	B8636-S023	
Sanderson, Mary B.	Moncton, NOK Kingston, ON	1884	Jun 8, 1916	B8636-S023	
Scott, Bessie Maud	Saint John	1882	Oct 12, 1918	B8712-S061	
Shaw, Agnes Amelia	Hartland	1883	Oct 15, 1918	B8814-S003 PA Esquimalt Military Hospital	
Shea, Catherine Regina	Saint John	1887	Apr 3, 1916	B8828-S030 Medaille d'Honneur	
Shepherd, Anna Isabel	Grand Manan	1887	Mar 28, 1917	B8843-S051	
Skillen, Mary Lucille	St. Martins, NOK Chicago	1890	Mar 15, 1917	B8961-S042 PA Manitoba	

Name	Birthplace	Year Born	Attestation Date	LAC File: Comments	School
Smith, Hazel May	Bloomfield	1879	Aug 28, 1916	B9055-S042 QAIMNS, 8 months	
Smith, Isadore Loretta	Fredericton	1885	Jul 5, 1918	B9062-S048	
Smith, Jessie Sara	Bathurst	1885	Jul 6, 1916	B9068-S054 Harvard, 12 months	
Smith, Nellie Graham	Harvey	1879	Jun 25, 1918	B9088-S021	
Stamers, Anna Irene	Saint John	1888	Jun 3, 1915	B9225-S032	SJSN 1913
Stannix, Jennie Fale	McAdam Junction	1886	Jun 10, 1918	B9235-S039 Harvard, ? months	
Steeves, Ina Maude	Salisbury	1890	Jul 23, 1918	B9263-S043	
Steeves, Paula Mae	Westmorland	1889	May 17, 1917	B9264-S003	
Steeves, Sarah Selina	Hillsborough	1888	Jan 27, 1917	B9264-S018	
Stevenson, Hilda Napier	Quebec City, NOK Fredericton	1890	Nov 30, 1916	B9294-S015	
Stewart, Eliza Mae	Bathurst, NOK Vancouver	1887	Mar 21, 1917	B9308-S001	
Stockton, Sylvia Octavia	Saint John, NOK Toronto	1888	Feb 12, 1918	B9345-S043	
Thompson, Alice Amelia	Chance Harbour	1884	Feb 4, 1915	B9621-S038	
Thompson, Mona Jane	Moncton, NOK Calgary	1890	Feb 3, 1917	B9651-S034 PA Calgary	

Name	Birthplace	Year Born	Attestation Date	LAC File: Comments	School
Turner, Millicent Aileen	Saint John	1889	Jul 8, 1918	B9841-S042	
Wallace, Mary Maud Theresa	Blacks Harbour	1887	Nov 8, 1915	B10039-S032	
Walsh, Mary Stewart	Moncton	1889	Apr 3, 1916	B10056-S038	McGill
Watling, Christina Mary	Chatham	1874	Apr 13, 1915	B10127-S013 RRC 2nd class	
West, Nina May	Moncton	1891	Jul 5, 1918	B10241-S030	
Wier, Beatrice Janet	Doaktown	1889	Mar 2, 1917	B10203-S062	
Wilson, Annie Lulu	Petersville	1886	Aug 16, 1916	B10434- S005	SJSN 1914
Wilson, Gertrude Clayton	Saint John	1890	Apr 1, 1916	B10449-S011	
Wilson, Lily Margot	East Glassville	1883	Dec 18, 1916	B10466-S039	
Wilson, Nella Myrtle (Matron)	Saint John	1885	Feb 3, 1915	B10467-S045 RRC lst class	SJSN 1907
Wishart, Joyce Thomson	Saint John, NOK Halifax	1888	Feb 4, 1915	B10509-S025	SJSN 1911
Woods, Margaret Jane	Welsford	1883	Apr 15, 1915	B10564-S013 RRC 2nd class	McGill
Wright, Mary Isobel	Restigouche County	1891	Jul 17, 1917	B10606-S061	

Note: The *Daily Gleaner* reported on May 28, 1917, that the sister of Sergeant Taylor (No. 8 Field Ambulance) was serving as a nursing sister with the Canadian forces in France and had died following an illness. There is no record of a Nursing Sister Taylor with a New Brunswick address or NOK in New Brunswick—perhaps she served with the British QAIMNS at the time of her death.

Other Nursing Sisters with a Connection to New Brunswick

Four nursing sisters were identified in New Brunswick newspapers or by other researchers, but, because of incomplete information, the New Brunswick connection is unclear or an LAC file could not be identified.

Name	Details
Sambel, Maud E.	Born in England, NOK in England, TOS in England; LAC File # B8622-S052
Samson, Bertha	Born in North Dakota, NOK Winnipeg, living in Manitoba; LAC File # B8624-S052
Sanders, Lucy	Born in Ontario, NOK Saskatchewan, living in Saskatchewan, enlisted in Alberta; LAC File # B8633-S009
Williams, Gertrude	Graduate of SJSN, identified by Alberta Hanscome as having served with the CAMC; no LAC file

Acknowledgements

I first learned about Nursing Sister Anna Stamers when I wrote an essay on *Llandovery Castle* for a History class with Dr. Marc Milner, then Director of the Gregg Centre for War and Society at the University of New Brunswick. Dr. Milner encouraged me to research Anna's story, otherwise I never would have started the project and certainly never would have finished it. In addition to Dr. Milner's encouragement and editing, Brent Wilson, Editor Emeritus at the Gregg Centre for the Study of War and Society, edited the manuscript, provided advice, obtained permissions to use the images I had located, and coordinated all interactions with the publisher, Goose Lane Editions. Brent arranged for Mike Bechthold to create maps to help the reader follow Anna's service in England and France. I also want to thank the staff of Goose Lane Editions, especially Julie Scriver and Alan Sheppard, and freelance copy editor Barry Norris, for their design expertise and editorial advice.

This book could not have been written without the foresight of many archivists and librarians who preserved, catalogued, and digitized original documents and newspapers to make them accessible for researchers. The records available through Library and Archives Canada and at http://heritage.canadiana.ca provide details of Anna's service. Saint John historian Harold Wright alerted me to the Militia and Defence files available at Heritage Canada, which were essential in following Anna's service in 1917, and provided several photos for the book. I relied heavily on the staff and librarians at the University of New Brunswick's Harriet Irving Library, including the technology staff, and they deserve my thanks for their interest, expertise, and forbearance. Finally, I want to thank my husband, Luke, for his patience while I spent hours researching and writing Anna's story. To my daughter, Tammy, and other family and friends who encouraged me when I doubted I would finish the project, I say "Thank You."

Selected Bibliography

Primary Sources

Anna's records with Militia and Defence, https://heritage.canadiana.ca/view/oocihm.lac_reel_t17641/1007?r=0&s=1.

Anna's service file at Library and Archives Canada, https://www.bac-lac.gc.ca/eng/discover/military-heritage/first-world-war/personnel-records/Pages/item.aspx?IdNumber=247238.

Census records, https://www.bac-lac.gc.ca/eng/census/Pages/census.aspx 1891, 1901, 1911, and 1921, https://automatedgenealogy.com.

"German War Trials: Judgment in Case of Lieutenants Dithmar and Boldt." *American Journal of International Law* 16, no. 4 (1922): 708-24, http://www.jstor.org/stable/2187594, accessed January 12, 2021.

Letter from Margaret Macdonald to W.R. Landon, May 12, 1922, http://www/bac-lac.gc.ca/eng/discover/military-heritage/first-world-war/canada-first-world-war/Pages/laura-gamble.aspx#b.

Letters of Helen Fowlds, http://digitalcollections.trentu.ca/exhibits/fowlds/.

Letters of Sophie Hoerner, https://www.bac-lac.gc.ca/eng/discover/military-heritage/first-world-war/canada-nursing-sisters/Pages/sophie-hoerner.aspx.

Map of hospitals, and Record of Service for Moore Barracks Hospital, No. 1 CGH, No. 16 CGH, and HMHS *Llandovery Castle*, https://www.canada.ca/en/department-national-defence/services/military-history/history-heritage/official-military-history-lineages/ledgers/ww1-medical-units.html.

Memorial Service Program, Toronto, July 14, 1918, https://www.canadiana.ca/view/oocihm.87320/1?r=0&s=1.

Moore Barracks Ledger, https://www.canada.ca/content/dam/themes/defence/caf/militaryhistory/dhh/ledgers/medical/no-11-canadian-general-hospital.jpg, accessed September 8, 2018.

Nominal Rolls, Nursing Sisters, 1914 and 1915, https://www.canadiana.ca /view/oocihm.9_09096/1?r=0&s=1; https://www.canadiana.ca /view/oocihm.9_10478; and https://archive.org/details/CEF_ NursingSistersDrafts_1915.

Ontario Stretcher, http://rcnarchive.rcn.org.uk/data/VOLUME073-1925 /page084-volume73-april1925.pdf.

Orpington General Hospital Ledger, https://www.canada.ca/content/dam /themes/defence/caf/militaryhistory/dhh/ledgers/medical/narrative -gen16.jpg, accessed August-September 2018.

Record of Service, CAMC Depot, https://www.canada.ca/content/dam /themes/defence/caf/militaryhistory/dhh/ledgers/medical/canadian -army-medical-corps-depot.jpg, accessed September 8, 2018.

Record of Service at Moore Barracks Hospital, No. 1 CGH, No. 16 CGH, HMHS *Llandovery Castle*, https://www.canada.ca/en/department -national-defence/services/military-history/history-heritage/official -military-history-lineages/ledgers/ww1-medical-units.html, and https:// www.canada.ca/content/dam/themes/defence/caf/militaryhistory/dhh /ledgers/medical/no-11-canadian-general-hospital.jpg.

Report on the Work of the C.A.M.C. Nursing Service with the B.E.F. in France, National Archives WO222/2134, http://www.scarlettfinders .co.uk/20.html.

Saint John General Hospital School of Nursing, Nursing Records Register, Graduates of General Public Hospital School for Nurses 1890-1919, Date of Admission and Graduation. New Brunswick Museum.

The Sinking of the H.M.H.S. Llandovery Castle, 1918. Ottawa: Director of Public Information, https://www.canadiana.ca/view /oocihm.8_06880_5/7?r=0&s=1.

War Diary, Moore Barracks Canadian Hospital, August 8, 1915-April 27, 1919, http://collectionscanada.gc.ca, accessed August 27, 2018.

Secondary Sources
Adami, J. George. *War Story of the Canadian Army Medical Corps*. London: Colour, 1918. Available at http://digital.library.upennb.edu/women /adami/camc/camc.html.

"As Sister on a Hospital Ship." *Canadian Nurse and Hospital Review*, June 1918.

Atenstaedt, R.L. "Trench Fever: The British Medical Response in the Great War." *Journal of the Royal Society of Medicine* 99 no. 11 (2006): 564-68.

Beaupré, Diane. "En Route to Flanders Fields: The Canadians at Shorncliffe during the Great War." *London Journal of Canadian Studies* 23 (2007-2008). Available at https://www.canadianukgravesww1.co.uk /pdf/enroutetoflandersfields-LJCS.pdf.

Beesly, Patrick. *Room 40: British Naval Intelligence, 1914-18*. London: Hamish Hamilton, 1982.

Cameron, Kenneth. *No. 1 Canadian General Hospital, 1914-1919: With a Record of the Work of the Medical Division by Norman B. Gwyn and a Note Upon the Treatment of Fracture of the Femur*. Sackville, NB: Tribune Press, 1938.

Campbell, John. *Medicine on the battlefield*. Available at http://www .ncpedia.org/ww1-medicine-battlefield.

Cook, Tim. "The Politics of Surrender: Canadian Soldiers and the Killing of Prisoners in the Great War." *Journal of Military History* 70, no. 3 (2006): 637-65.

Demers, Daniel J. "The Sinking of Llandovery Castle." *Canadian Naval Review* 11, no. 2 (2015): 25-28. Available at http://www.navalreview.ca /2015/10/the-sinking-of-llandovery-castle/.

Dewar, Katherine. *Those Splendid Girls. The Heroic Service of Prince Edward Island Nurses in the Great War*. Charlottetown: Island Studies Press, 2014.

Doucet, Jay, Gregory Haley, and Vivian McAllister. "Massacre of CAMC Personnel after the Sinking of HMHS *Llandovery Castle* and the Evolution of Modern War Crime Jurisprudence." *Canadian Journal of Surgery* 61, no. 3 (2018): 155-57. Available at http://www.gwpda.org /naval/lcastl10.html.

Duffus, Maureen. *Battlefront Nurses in WWI: The Canadian Army Medical Corps in England, France, and Salonika, 1914-1919*. Victoria, BC: Town and Gown Press, 2009.

Evans, Suzanne. "History of the Silver Cross Medal." *Canadian Military*

History 19, no. 1: article 5. Available at https://scholars.wlu.ca
/cmh/vol19/iss1/5, 2010.

Fitzgerald, Gerard J. "Chemical Warfare and Medical Response during
World War I." *American Journal of Public Health* 98, no. 4 (2008):
611-25.

Hallett, Christine E. *Containing Trauma: Nursing Work in the First World
War*. Manchester: Manchester University Press, 2009.

———. *Veiled Warriors: Allied Nurses of the First World War*. Oxford: Oxford
University Press, 2014.

Hanscome, A.V. *History of the Saint John General Hospital and School of
Nursing*. Saint John, NB: Lingley Printing, 1955.

"The Hospital Ship Llandovery Castle. Editorial." *Canadian Medical
Association Journal* 8, no. 8 (1918): 734-36.

Johnson, Jonathan. *Canadian Military Hospitals at Sea 1914-1919*. Available
at https://www.royalcdnmedicalsvc.ca/wp-content/uploads/2015/01
/CANADIAN-HOSPITAL-SHIPS-1914-19.pdf.

Jones, Kierra. "On Tour: Their Votes Counted." *Canadian Nurse*, July 3,
2017. Available at https://canadian-nurse.com/en/articles/issues/2017
/july-august-2017/on-tour-their-votes-counted.

Macphail, Andrew. *Official History of the Canadian Forces in the Great War
1914-19: The Medical Services*. Ottawa: F.A. Acland, King's Printer, 1925.

Mann, Susan, ed. *The War Diary of Clare Gass 1915-1918*. Montreal;
Kingston, ON: McGill-Queen's University Press, 2000.

McGreal, Stephen. *The War on Hospital Ships, 1914-1918*. Barnsley, UK:
Pen & Sword Maritime, 2009.

McKenzie, Andrea, ed. *War-Torn Exchanges: The Lives and Letters of
Nursing Sisters Laura Holland and Mildred Forbes*. Vancouver: UBC
Press, 2016.

Morton, Desmond. *When Your Number's Up: The Canadian Soldier in the
First World War*. Toronto: Random House of Canada, 1993.

Nicholson, Gerald W.L. *Canada's Nursing Sisters*. Toronto: S. Stevens, 1975.

Norris, Marjorie. *Sister Heroines: The Roseate Glow of Wartime Nursing
1914-1918*. Calgary: Bunker to Bunker Publishing, 2002.

"Nursing Contingent of the Canadian Expeditionary Force." *British Journal of Nursing*, October 24, 1914, 325.

Patton, James. "Gas in the Great War." *Medicine in the First World War.* Kansas City: University of Kansas Medical Center, n.d. Available at https://www.kumc.edu/wwi/medicine/gas-in-the-great-war. html#:~:text=Gas%20in%20The%20Great%20War%20James%20 Patton%2C%20BS,one%20agent%20of%20offensive%20effort%2C %20an%20artillery%20round.

Quinn, Shawna M. *Agnes Warner and the Nursing Sisters of the Great War.* Fredericton, NB: New Brunswick Military Heritage Project and Goose Lane Editions, 2010.

"The Sinking of the Llandovery Castle." *British Medical Journal* 2, no. 3022 (1918): 294.

Snell, A.E. *The C.A.M.C. with the Canadian Corps During the Last Hundred Days of the Great War.* Ottawa: F.A. Acland, King's Printer, 1924. Available at https://www.canada.ca/en/department-national-defence /services/military-history/history-heritage/official-military-history -lineages/official-histories/book-1924-medical-corps.html.

Solis, Gary D. "Obedience of Orders and the Law of War: Judicial Application in American Forums." *American University International Law Review* 15, no. 2 (1999): 481-526. Available at http:// digitalcommons.wcl.american.edu.auilr\.

Toman, Cynthia. *Sister Soldiers of the Great War: The Nurses of the Canadian Army Medical Corps.* Vancouver: UBC Press, 2016.

United Kingdom. Foreign Office. "Correspondence with the German Government regarding the Alleged Misuse of British Hospital Ships." London: H.M. Stationary Office, 1917.

———. House of Commons. Debate, February 17, 1916, vol. 80, cc 238-40. Available at https://api.parliament.uk/historic-hansard /commons/1916/feb/17/shorncliffe-camp-moore-barracks.

"The War on Hospital Ships from the Narratives of Eye-Witnesses." London: T. Fisher Unwin, 1917.

Wilson, Woodrow. "Address of the President of the United States." Senate Documents, 65th Congress, First Session. Washington, DC: US Government Printing Office, 1917. Available at http://wps.prenhall

.com/wps/media/objects/107/110495/ch22_a2_d1.pdf ; accessed April 5, 2015.

Wilson-Simmie, Katharine. *Lights Out: The Memoir of Nursing Sister Kate Wilson, Canadian Army Medical Corps, 1915-1917*. Ottawa: CEF Books, 2003.

Newspapers

Chronicle Herald (Halifax)

Daily Colonist (Victoria, BC)

Daily Gleaner (Fredericton)

Daily Telegraph and The Sun (Saint John)

Daily Times (Moncton)

Evening Times-Globe (Saint John)

Evening Times and Star (Saint John)

Gazette (Montreal)

Globe (Toronto)

Messenger and Visitor (Saint John)

Moncton Transcript

Otago Daily Times (Dunedin, New Zealand)

Ottawa Citizen

Saint John Globe

Standard (Saint John)

Telegraph Journal (Saint John)

Times (London)

Index

References in **bold** refer to images

A

Adami, J. George 87
Addy, Mrs. John (Gladys Stamers, sister) 18, 19, 21, 120, 169
Alwyn huts 87
ambulances 39, 58, **60**, 73
Amiens, Battle of 153
amputations 34, 104, 125
Araguaya 138, 140
Armstrong, Florence Mary 49
Arras, Battle of 103
"asleep in the deep" (MacLatchy) 184
Asturias 131, 134, 135

B

Babbitt, Miss 46
Baker, Albert 163
Baldwin, Dorothy 142
Balloch, Pauline 139
Barton, Irene 49, 86
Barton, Lena M. 55
Barton, Sister 96
Beauchesne, F. 115
Beaupré, Diane 62
Benne, Jean 122
Bennett-Goldney, Francis 67
Binyon, Lawrence 184
blackout conditions 53, 63
blood transfusions 34
Bluebirds 42
Boldt, John 145, 154-55
bombings
    on Folkestone 108
    on Moore Barracks 62
    on No. 1 CGH 91, 143, 159
    on No. 1 GHS 141

on No. 3 CSH 142
Bonar Law, Andrew 68, 116, 150
Bongard, Ella Mae 123
Borden, Robert 120, 153
Boulogne, France 59
Brindle, W. 159
British Expeditionary Force (BEF) 96
British Medical Journal 131
Brown, Mildred 113
Brussels Street Baptist Church 20, 160

C

Cameron, Kenneth
    on cost of uniforms 42
    on flow of patients 72, 90, 92, 95, 97-99, 104
    on No. 1 CGH 81, 86-87, 90, 107
    on patient conditions 72, 84
    on social functions and events 92, 96, 101
    on staff 94, 100
    on weather conditions 89, 101
Campbell, Miss 137
Canadian Army Medical Corps (CAMC)
    about 44, 51, 58, 92, 122
    acceptance announcements 46
    Anna in 29, 48, 57, 108, 127
    bed capacity 29
    instructions for nursing sisters 69
    Military Selection Committee 41
    New Brunswick nurses in 10, 29, 43, 185
    number of nurses 10, 40, 44, 179
    official war diaries 11
    personnel 9, 29, 44, 57
    services held for dead 159
    Training Depot 62
    uniforms **41**, 41-42, 51

The New Brunswick Military Heritage Project

The New Brunswick Military Heritage Project, a non-profit organization devoted to public awareness of the remarkable military heritage of the province, is an initiative of the Brigadier Milton F. Gregg, VC, Centre for the Study of War and Society of the University of New Brunswick. The organization consists of museum professionals, teachers, university professors, graduate students, active and retired members of the Canadian Forces, and other historians. We welcome public involvement. People who have ideas for books or information for our database can contact us through our website: www.unb.ca/nbmhp.

One of the main activities of the New Brunswick Military Heritage Project is the publication of the New Brunswick Military Heritage Series with Goose Lane Editions. This series of books is under the direction of J. Brent Wilson, Director of the New Brunswick Military Heritage Project at the University of New Brunswick. Publication of the series is supported by a grant from the Province of New Brunswick and the Canadian War Museum.

The New Brunswick Military History Series

Volume 1
Saint John Fortifications, 1630-1956,
Roger Sarty and Doug Knight

Volume 2
Hope Restored: The American Revolution and the
Founding of New Brunswick, Robert L. Dallison

Volume 3
The Siege of Fort Beauséjour, 1755, Chris M. Hand

Volume 4
Riding into War: The Memoir of a Horse Transport Driver,
1916-1919, James Robert Johnston

Volume 5
The Road to Canada: The Grand Communications Route
from Saint John to Quebec, W.E. (Gary) Campbell

Volume 6
Trimming Yankee Sails: Pirates and Privateers
of New Brunswick, Faye Kert

Volume 7
War on the Home Front: The Farm Diaries
of Daniel MacMillan, 1914-1927,
edited by Bill Parenteau and Stephen Dutcher

About the Author

Dianne Kelly holds a BBA, MBA, and a BA in history from the University of New Brunswick, the latter completed upon her retirement from the New Brunswick provincial civil service. She received the Malleson Prize in Imperial and Commonwealth Military History for her essay on the sinking of the HMHS *Llandovery Castle*. Inspired by her studies and trips to First and Second World War battlefields in Europe, Kelly became interested in the story of Nursing Sister Anna Stamers, who died with other nursing sisters on the HMHS *Llandovery Castle*. Outside of her research, Kelly has held numerous positions with the New Brunswick Provincial Government, including Chief Firearms Officer, Chief Coroner, and Director of Consumer Affairs.